This edition is limited to
one thousand copies of which
this is number 967

Robert Adams

The life and work of

ALEXANDER BERCOVITCH
ARTIST

by Robert Adams

Editions Marlowe
Montreal

Printing : Groupe Litho Graphique P.P.S.D. Inc.
Phototypesetting : Entreprises Précigraphes ltée
Colour transparencies : Al Kilbertus

Distribution : Editions Marlowe
C.P. 603
5751 Sherbrooke Street West
Montréal, Québec
H4A 3R1

Dépôt légal : Bibliothèque Nationale du Canada ISBN 0-9693439-0-6
2ᵉ trimestre 1988

This book is for my wife
Pearl Brownstein Adams

Patrons

Sylvia Bercovitch Ary

Eytan Bercovitch

Gila Bercovitch

Sacvan Bercovitch

Beatrice and Joseph Flamer

Dr. and Mrs. Hirsh Rosenfeld

Mr. and Mrs. Saul Shapiro

and
in memory of

Joseph Achtman

Harry Brownstein

Samuel Chait Q.C.

The research for the biography was funded by a grant from the
Jewish Community Foundation of Greater Montreal

Table of Contents

Introduction

Many of the details of Bercovitch's personal life are from the oral history of his family. This history was recorded in many hours of interviews with his daughter, the Canadian painter Sylvia Ary, and his son, Sacvan Bercovitch, Professor of English and American Literature at Harvard University. The interviews took place in Montreal between November 1986 and January 1988. Where corroboration is available it will be indicated.

Acknowledgements

I owe the greatest debt to my wife Pearl for her loving encouragement, her invaluable and insightful suggestions, her editing and proof-reading, and her confidence in me when I hesitated.

To Sylvia, whose work my wife and I have admired and collected for so long, and to Sacvan, I offer my gratitude for their constant support, their careful reading of the manuscript at each stage of the writing, and their friendship. I must also express my appreciation to Gila Bercovitch for her close reading of the text and for her many helpful comments, to Jack J. Gordon for his anecdotes and infectious enthusiasm, and to ninety-five private collectors in Eastern Canada for their kindness in allowing me into their homes to photograph and to study paintings by Bercovitch.

I would like to acknowledge the generous cooperation of the following people : Mme. Androussenko of the Soviet Academy of Arts and Science ; Abe Bogen of Jewish Immigrant Aid Services, Montreal ; René Buisson, Founder and President of the Musée Marc-Aurèle Fortin ; François-Marc Gagnon, Professor of Art History at the Université de Montréal ; Charles Hill, Curator of Canadian Art at the National Gallery, Ottawa ; the movie historian Dane Lanken ; the Montreal historian Allan Raymond ; and Esther Trépanier, Professor of Art History at the Université du Québec à Montréal.

For translation from Russian I am grateful to Shalom Labkovsky, and for translation from Yiddish to Sylvia Ary, Abe Bogen, and David Rome.

To those who knew Bercovitch, and were good enough to share their memories with me, I can only say that, without their assistance, my task would have been impossible. I am particularly indebted to the following, and I ask them to accept my thanks.

Ethel Achtman
Ida & Harry Allister
Sally Allister
Solomon Ary
Bea Bazar
Irving Bernstein
Anita Billick
Judith Borenstein
Madeleine Boyer
Rita Briansky
Ghitta Caiserman-Roth
Luba Chaitman
Norman Cohen
Howard Daum
Camille de Guise
Zave Ettinger
Henry Eveleigh
Malca Friedman
Eudice Garmaise

Joffre Gendron
Edith Gold
Regina Seiden Goldberg
Abe Gordon
Harold B. Gordon
Jack J. Gordon
Esther Handel
Allan Harrison
Hyman Hershman
Sophie Mayman Heyden
Rose Mamelak Johnstone
Freda & Gershon Kaplan
François Lanoue c.s.v.
Pearl Leibovitch
Jonas London
Helen Maron
Florence Millman
Louis Muhlstock
Zelda & Jerome Myers

Rosalie Namer
Blanche Parent
Morton Pesner
Alfred Pinsky
Sol Pomerance
Ruth & Philip Pressman
Lilian Reinblatt
David Rome
Morris Rudin
Trudy Sack
Elsie Salomons
Gedalia Schacter
David Schulman
Harold Segall
Saul Shapiro
David Silverberg
Regina Shoolman Slatkin
Max Stern
Esther Wertheimer

The thirty-seven colour plates chosen for this volume were selected to illustrate the diversity of Bercovitch's interests and his willingness to experiment. They present, I believe, a fair over-view of his *oeuvre* between 1922 and 1951, without any undue emphasis on any one period.

Robert Adams
Montreal, February 1988.

List of Plates

16. **"Val Morin — Lake and Trees"** c. 1936
oil on board, 50 x 70 cm. Harold B. Gordon

17. **"Sue Boroff"** c. 1935
oil on cloth on board, 102 x 59 cm. Judith Borenstein

18. **"Assya"** c. 1935
oil on paper on board, 34 x 28 cm. Private collection

19. **"Boat in Harbour"** c. 1936
gouache on paper, 35 x 50 cm. Dr. & Mrs. David T. Shizgal

20. **"Der Stumer"** (The Mute) 1936
pencil and crayon on cardboard, 30 x 23 cm. Private collection

21. **"Two Huts on Beach near Percé"** 1937
oil on board, 43 x 60 cm. Jack J. Gordon

22. **"Percé — the Poverty of the Land"** c. 1937
gouache on paper, 58 x 80 cm. Mr. & Mrs. Saul Shapiro

23. **"Laurier Avenue"** 1933
gouache on paper, 50 x 70 cm. Mr. & Mrs. Saul Shapiro

24. **"Laurentian Snow Scene"** c. 1938
oil on board, 52 x 66 cm. Private collection

25. **"Montreal Street"** c. 1939
gouache on paper, 17 x 25 cm. Ethel Achtman

26. **"Der Oytzer"** (The Treasure) 1939
gouache and pastel on paper, 44 x 85 cm. Harold B. Gordon

27. **"The Two Gangsters"** 1940
oil on board, 68 x 54 cm. Private collection

28. **"Gaspé: Cliff and Sea"** c. 1940
watercolour on paper, 44 x 58 cm. Private collection

29. **"Untitled Nude"** 1942
pastel on paper, 110 x 58 cm. Mr. & Mrs. Saul Shapiro

30. **"Petrushka"** 1946
oil on gold paint on canvas, 200 x 478 cm. Jack J. Gordon

31. **"Moishele Geller, Cantor"** 1946
oil on board, 95 x 58 cm. Harold B. Gordon

32. **"Eve"** 1948
book illustration, 20 x 15 cm. Mr. & Mrs. Saul Shapiro

33. **"Negress"** 1948
book illustration, 20 x 15 cm. Mr. & Mrs. Saul Shapiro

34. **"Mount Royal in Fall"** c. 1948
oil on cloth, 56 x 72 cm. Jack J. Gordon

35. **"Two Brothers"** 1949
oil on canvas, 86 x 78 cm. Mr. & Mrs. Saul Shapiro

36. **"Harold Gordon"** 1949
pastel on paper, 68 x 55 cm. Harold B. Gordon

37. **"Street in Québec City"** c. 1950
pastel on paper, 39 x 58 cm. Pinnie & Jack Gordon

The Formative Years: Kherson, Jerusalem, St. Petersburg, Munich, Odessa, Moscow.

Alexander Bercovitch[1] died of a heart attack on a Montreal street on January 7, 1951. He was fifty-nine years old and a gifted artist, and he was penniless. He was on his way to the opening of a major exhibition of his paintings, the first he had had in ten years.

His harsh journey had begun on March 15, 1891,[2] in the port city of Kherson, near Odessa in the Ukraine. Kherson was in the Pale of Settlement, that area defined by the Tsars for more than a century as the only region in which Russian Jews might live. By 1891 nearly five million Jews, half of the world's Jewish population, lived in the Pale, often squeezed by the authorities into cities like Kherson for easier policing.[3] Here on the western edge of the Russian Empire Jews might go about their business, under Russian control but far from the delicately Christian heart of Holy Mother Russia.

Bercovitch was born into the family of a shoemaker considered poor and unlucky even by the undemanding standards of the Jews of Kherson. Yeshua and Velya Bercovitch had already produced six children. The daughters, Sonya, Chava, and Chaya, had survived, but the three sons had all died in infancy of infections following circumcision.

When Alexander was born, his parents took the precaution of calling him "Alter" (old man) in an effort to ward off the Evil Eye. The name would also be, they hoped, a self-fulfilling prophecy. To many in the family Alexander would always remain "Alter", though he himself used "Alexander" and, for his friends, the diminutive "Sasha".

In 1898, at the age of seven, Alexander was apprenticed to a bookbinder. There he would learn a trade and receive room and board, but he found the learning and lodging insufficient compensation for the frequent beatings and ran home in the following year. By this time he had a slight stutter, a mild speech impediment that he was never to lose. Before the beatings, he had already been suffering from recurring nightmares about a big fire, part of a local pogrom, which he had seen two years earlier.[4] The bookbinder's beatings both intensified the nightmares and brought about the stammer in his speech.

His father made no further attempt to apprentice him, and Alexander, a sickly child, was allowed to stay home.

At the age of nine he had the experience which decided the direction of his life. Through a grill in the wall of a Kherson monastery, he saw the monks engaged in the painting of ikons. The monks saw him watching, hour after hour, day after day. After a while they asked him to run errands, and allowed him inside the walls, for longer and longer periods at a time. They were amused by the little Jewish boy's fascination with ikons and he became their mascot. Finally they gave him paint and a few words of instruction. Thus began an informal and irregular apprenticeship that lasted for nearly six years. The boy's activity violated all his family's religious prohibitions, but his father found it impossible to deny his only son what quickly became a passion for him. For their part, the Kherson monks were amazed at the boy's talent and at his eagerness to master a craft that was completely alien to his culture. There had been little evidence of creative talent in any other member of the family. Velya Bercovitch had had the habit of cutting out intricate paper patterns, but custom and religious law had prevented her from any more ambitious activity in the creative field.

By 1906, at the age of 15, Alexander had achieved local recognition as an artist. The ban on Yiddish theatre[5] had been relaxed and he was painting sets and designing costumes for local theatrical productions. The Jewish residents of the overcrowded cities of the Pale compensated for their poverty by a frenzy of creative life and the talents of the young Alexander Bercovitch were much in demand. He was able to accumulate the staggering sum of 200 roubles[6] at a time when a Jewish artisan might work 90 hours in a week for as little as three roubles.[7] He dreamed of studying at the St. Petersburg Academy, but there were restrictions on residence. The only Jews permitted to live outside the Pale, in cities like Moscow and St. Petersburg, were lawyers, health professionals, and wealthy merchants (of the First Guild), whose collective purse was continually called upon to succour the Jewish poor. In 1906 nearly one-half of Russia's Jews were kept alive by the charity of their co-religionists.[8] However, no one was safe : even the favoured few lived precariously. The great Léon Bakst, born Lev Rosenberg of a rich merchant family, had already been expelled from the St. Petersburg Academy for painting a Holy Family with physical features that might be thought Jewish. Bakst was lucky to have been a favourite of the Grand Duke Vladimir, whose children he tutored, or the blasphemy might have received a more severe sanction than expulsion.[9]

St. Petersburg was out of the question for the young Bercovitch, but early in 1907 there came news from the outside world that solved the problem of where he might receive further training.

Several months earlier, Boris Schatz, formerly the Court Sculptor of Ferdinand of Bulgaria, had founded a new art school in Jerusalem. The aim of the new Bezalel School of Art was to foster in Palestine and in the Diaspora a Jewish national style in the arts that would combine European techniques with Middle Eastern art forms.[10]

The project aroused tremendous interest in Zionist circles, and a grant from Kherson benefactors, together with his own considerable savings, enabled Bercovitch to go to Jerusalem to study under Schatz.[11]

He spent more than three years in Palestine. In later life he rarely spoke about those years except to say that he had been happy at the school, that he had acquired the basic techniques he needed, and that he had learned to love quiet places.

In 1910 he returned to Kherson and exhibited for the first time.[12] The event was Vladimir Izdeb-

sky's Second International Salon in Odessa. It was here that Bercovitch befriended David Burliuk who, with his brother Vladimir and Natalia Goncharova, had already launched the Russian Primitivist movement in 1909 at the Third "Golden Fleece" Exhibition at St. Petersburg. Burliuk had come back to Odessa in 1910 to be with his ailing father, and would spend nearly two years there before going to Moscow to co-found, with Mayakovsky, the Russian Futurist movement.[13] (Letters written later by Burliuk to Bercovitch suggest that they did not see each other after 1911 — see Appendix 1.)

The Russia of 1910 was a paradox of creativity and repression. Miserably and fatally backward politically, it was wonderfully progressive in the arts. This had been particularly true since 1899, when Diaghilev, with Bakst, Benois, and Dobujinsky, had founded the group "Mir Iskusstva" (World of Art), together with the review of the same name. As Bercovitch put it himself, "Russians were the first to embrace the important modern movements in painting... Cézanne, Picasso, and the rest of the post-Impressionists were first appreciated in Russia... before they were popularly accepted, even in Paris."[14]

The new influences were seen not only in St. Petersburg and Moscow, but in provincial centres like Kiev, Kharkov, and Odessa.[15] "Hardly had Italian Futurism been proclaimed in Milan than it was reflected in Moscow and St. Petersburg."[16]

Bercovitch was aware of both Primitivism and the move to Futurism, but he had already begun to develop his own very distinctive style. It combined the vibrant stillness of the ikon, the energy of passion forever enclosed in the moment, with a willingness to experiment with form-building that came with a knowledge of what Cézanne was doing. To this was added the love of strong, clear forms that he had brought back from Palestine, even before he was exposed to the power and simplicity of his friend Burliuk's work. Bercovitch's talent would come to full flowering twelve years later in Russian Turkestan, but his portfolio in Odessa was already of a standard to win him the Dr. Nathan Strauss Scholarship.[17] The scholarship was to be taken up at the Munich Academy, but, before he left for Germany, Bercovitch decided to risk a stay in St. Petersburg.

Since he was denied entry into the Academy, he enrolled at the much smaller Bakst-Dobujinsky school. It was the same school at which Chagall had studied briefly in 1909.[18] Bercovitch's stay was short : he had no powerful protector and a contravention of the residence restrictions carried a heavy penalty. He did, however, succeed in helping with the preparation of the décor of *Scheherazade*. Bakst was preparing the sets to be shipped to Paris for the coming triumph of the Ballet Russe de Diaghilev. The brief association was a source of lifelong pride to Bercovitch.[19]

In 1911 he took up the Strauss scholarship in Munich, where he came under the influence of Lovis Corinth and Franz von Stuck.[20] Stuck, who painted in the allegorical style of Böcklin, was the same professor who, eleven years earlier, had given Kandinsky his basic training in European Realism before Kandinsky left Stuck, the Academy, and Realism to make his own way to the creation of the world's first abstract painting in 1910.[21]

From Stuck, Bercovitch learned fundamentals. From Corinth, under whom he studied before Corinth left Munich for Berlin, he learned to take risks. Corinth was himself relearning to paint, with his left hand, after a stroke.[22] With his guidance, Bercovitch began to look for simpler forms and new rhythms. He began to break his perceptions into their component parts and to accentuate the most poignant. The Expressionist elements in his work date from those days with Stuck and Corinth.

The First World War compelled him to return to Kherson. He was 23 years old in 1914 and soon a conscript in the Tsar's army, but his military career was brief. Within months he had deserted. Within weeks thereafter he had a very heavy beard. For the next three years, until the Revolution, he lived in hiding. For a part of the time he was sheltered by the family of Bryna Avrutick, who was later to become his second wife. She was beautiful and five years his junior; but, although they were attracted to each other, nothing more serious than a physical relationship developed at the time. Bercovitch, a permanent skeptic, was apolitical, and Bryna was a Communist. She was quite prepared to give aid and comfort to a deserter from an imperialist struggle, but the whole of her being was committed to the coming Revolution.

Bryna Avrutick, 18 years old in 1914, was a remarkable woman. Her father had died when she was nine, but she had been able to finish "gymnasium" (academic high school). She had obtained lessons in Russian, and the money for her school fees, from a doctor's family. In return she did housework. She had made the arrangement herself before her tenth birthday. By October 1917, she was not only literate but widely read in both Yiddish and Russian, and a member of the Jewish intellectual movement. She had also expelled Alexander Bercovitch from the Avrutick home after she discovered that he was having an affair with her best friend. In 1917 she joined the Red Army to fight to protect the Revolution. In 1919 she was wounded while fighting on the Polish front and hospitalized. Conditions were primitive and she caught typhus. It was not until 1920 that she returned, emaciated, to Kherson. (For her own very moving account of her homecoming and her mother's reaction, see Appendix 2.)

Bercovitch in the meantime had been busy. With the Revolution came an end to the restrictions of the Pale, and in early 1918 he left Odessa, where he had been living since his expulsion from the Avrutick home in Kherson, and went to Moscow to paint. But there were no funds to maintain him and by the following year he was back in Kherson with his parents.

Bryna Avrutick had gone off to fight for her truth, and Bercovitch became interested in another young woman from Kherson, Baila V'Dovetz. They had met earlier during his period of hiding while she was studying music at the Odessa Conservatory.[23] After a brief courtship, they married.

They were happy, but the world outside pressed hard upon them. Baila remembers that "the economic situation in Russia soon after the Revolution was very difficult... We were very poor. There were days when we didn't have a piece of bread."[24]

It was not that Bercovitch had no work: there were simply no resources with which to pay him.

"He was painting the stage decorations for the Odessa Opera. I remember how beautiful the stage sets were for the performance of *Rusalka* [the 1856 opera by Dargomyzhsky]... he painted with every nerve and fibre of his being."[25]

A son, Kalmushe, was born on April 29, 1920, and poverty forced the young couple back to Kherson to live with the artist's parents.

By the fall of 1920 the poverty was so acute that Bercovitch went alone to Moscow to find work. Within weeks he was employed in the theatre and sent for Baila. She feared the long journey with an infant and the terrible Moscow frosts, and did not follow her husband that first winter. They never saw each other again.[26]

In Moscow, Bercovitch had found work at the Habima, a Hebrew theatre affiliated with the Moscow Art Theatre. The Habima had emerged from the post-Revolutionary chaos in a Moscow now open to Jews. The guiding genius of the young theatre was the Armenian director Vachtangov, and to his productions came all the great figures of the Moscow theatre world, including Stanislavsky and Meyerhold.[27] As a Moscow theatre, the Habima was under the direct supervision of Kandinsky himself.[28]

The greatest triumph of the Habima was Vachtangov's 1922 *Princess Turandot*, a Hebrew version of the eighteenth century drama by Carlo Gozzi.[29] The set designer was Yignat Nivinsky, assisted by Alexander Bercovitch.[30]

At this time Bercovitch and Bryna Avrutick met again. After the victory of the Red Army against both the counter-revolution and the intervention of the capitalist countries, Bryna had been demobilised. She had come to Moscow to study theatre under the director Meyerhold, whose political commitment to minimizing individuality on stage suited Bryna's political views.[31]

The Revolution accomplished and Bercovitch's indiscretion with Bryna's friend sufficiently in the past, they were drawn together by a shared interest in the theatre. They set up house together and could have married. Bercovitch was now free, having divorced Baila the year before.[32] It was Bryna who found a ceremony unnecessary: it was, she thought, a bourgeois concept, and Bercovitch, never one to welcome constraint, acquiesced.

They might have fared badly: these were hard times in Russia. The Civil War was hardly over, and the defeat of the interventionist forces had been costly. In the two preceding years, all four of Bryna's brothers had left Russia for the New World. One, Shoil, had gone to New York, while the other three, Yankel, Fischel, and Nachman, had all settled in Montreal to become, respectively, a blacksmith, a shochet, and a Yiddish teacher.[33] The brothers had a vivid memory of the hunger they had escaped from, and, as soon as they found work, they hastened to send food parcels to their sister. In a starving Moscow, she and Bercovitch could scarcely believe their good fortune. Those items that weren't eaten were easily exchanged for other necessities, or sold. The bounty from Montreal meant that they were a couple to be envied.

The idyll ended in the fall of 1922 when Bryna announced that she was pregnant. Bercovitch demanded that she have an abortion, easily available at the time. He had not long before seen the last of one family and he wasn't anxious to start another.

The confrontation was hysterical on both sides. Bryna threw him out and he did not try to return. He had somewhere to go.

Kandinsky, whom he knew through the Habima, had told him about the new art schools being set up in the various republics,[34] and Bercovitch had some particular knowledge of Soviet Turkestan. He had worked on the decoration of the Republic's pavilion at a 1922 industrial exhibition, and he knew that there were vacant positions at the new school in Ashkabad.

At the same time, he had just received notice that he had been accepted at the Stigliz Academy in Leningrad.[35] (The Stigliz would be incorporated into the Leningrad Academy of Fine Arts in 1923.)

It was a difficult decision for Bercovitch to make, whether to study in Leningrad or to teach in Ashkabad. He decided at first in favour of the former and went, without Bryna, to study at the Stigliz under the professors Carov and Denisov.[36]

In the late fall of 1922, he reversed his decision and applied for a teaching post in Ashkabad. It is not possible to know the reason for the change of heart. Madame Androussenko of the Soviet Academy of Arts and Science speculates that he might have anticipated a problem because of the projected merger of the Stigliz with the Leningrad Academy.[37] His schooling, especially that period spent at the Bezalel in Jerusalem, did not correspond to the normal gymnasium-centred preparation required by the Academy.

Whatever the reason, Bercovitch left Leningrad in 1922. He went to Ashkabad to teach, and he went alone.

---

1. The Russian passport issued on 19 May 1926 gives his name as Alexandre Sinowiewitch Berkowitch (see Appendix 4). The middle name is not a patronymic since Bercovitch's father was Yeshua, and since a Jew would not normally carry the name of a living parent. The name had been assigned arbitrarily in Bercovitch's youth by a Russian official who needed to fill the three standard spaces on a Russian form. The pronunciation of his first name by his family is best reflected in the spelling "Alexander", although the artist used various spellings in English, both on documents and in signing his work. "Aleksandre", "Alexandre", and "Alexander" can all be found in the catalogues of the Spring Exhibitions of the Art Association of Montreal between 1927 and 1950. In Canada, his family name was always shown as "Bercovitch".

2. The date is that shown on his 1926 passport.

3. Martin Gilbert, *The Jews of Russia* (London: National Council for Soviet Jewry, 1976), p. 19, and Irving Howe, *World of Our Fathers* (N.Y.: Harcourt, Bryce, Jovanovich, 1976), p. 5. The Pale was composed of Lithuania, White Russia, the annexed Polish regions, and the Ukraine. Russia felt that it needed the Jews for economic reasons, but feared their presence if they came too near to the Russian heartland. It was Catherine the Great in the eighteenth century who found an answer to the problem, as non-Jewish Russians perceived it, and established the Pale.

4. For a full investigation of a "typical" Ukrainian pogrom, with particular reference to the role of the church, see Michael

Davitt, *Within the Pale* (Philadelphia : Jewish Publication Society, 1903).

5. For a full description of the restrictions on Russian Jews, see Howe, *World of Our Fathers*, p. 6, and Victoria Secunda, *Bei Mir Bist Du Schon* (N.Y.: Magic Circle Press, 1982), pp. 16-17. Russian Jewry had fared badly throughout the nineteenth century, with the reign of Nicholas I (1825-1855) a special nightmare. Among his more than 600 anti-Jewish decrees were those that permitted the expulsion of Jews from their traditional villages and the conscription of Jewish boys into the army for up to 25 years. His successor, Alexander II, was less severe, but Alexander III (1881-1894) declared of his Jewish subjects that he would convert a third, starve a third, and let the rest emigrate. Under Nicholas II (1894-1918), the situation worsened, especially after the 1905 defeat by the Japanese and the internal social unrest of the same year. The Jew was once again the scapegoat. Jews were seen as the core of the reform movement, and the "Black Hundreds", that loose confederation of anti-semitic Russian societies, received heavy subsidies from the Tsarist secret police. Pogroms became increasingly frequent.

6. Information given by Bercovitch in an interview with the *Montreal Daily Herald*, 7 April 1933. He also worked as a sign-painter in this period, 1906-07, according to Mrs. Luba Chaitman (interviewed in Montreal, 19 April 1987). Born Luba Belansman, she had known Bercovitch before she left Kherson for Canada in 1907. Her father had taught Bercovitch in "cheder" (Hebrew elementary school), and her brother Yehuda had worked briefly with Bercovitch as a commercial artist.

7. Salo Baron, *The Russian Jews Under Tsars and Soviets* (N.Y.: McMillan, 1976), pp. 113-114.

8. Secunda, *Bei Mir*, p. 4, and Gilbert, *Jews of Russia*, p. 25.

9. See, inter alia, "Leon Bakst," *Encyclopaedia Britannica*, 1974.

10. See "Boris Schatz," *Encyclopaedia Judaica*, 1971.

11. At this point, the oral history as related by the artist's children is confirmed by Bercovitch's first wife, Baila V'Dovetz, in a conversation recorded between her and Sylvia Ary in Israel in August 1977. She had known both Bercovitch and his parents in Kherson.

12. Ibid.

13. Camilla Gray, *The Great Experiment : Russian Art, 1863-1922* (N.Y.: Abrams, 1962), pp. 87, 288. During his stay in Odessa, and while he was studying at the Odessa Academy, Burliuk found time to exhibit both at the 1910 "Knave of Diamonds" Exhibition in Moscow, and at the first Blue Rider Exhibition in Munich.

14. Bercovitch, *Montreal Daily Herald*, 7 April 1933.

15. George Heard Hamilton, *Pelican History of Art* (London : Penguin, 1967), p. 305.

16. Werner Haftman, *Chagall* (N.Y.: Abrams, 1984), p. 13.

17. Biographical information supplied by Alexander Bercovitch to the Canadian National Gallery Archives, 16 June 1942.

18. Hamilton, *Pelican History of Art*, p. 435.

19. Moe Reinblatt, "Aleksandre Bercovitch," *Canadian Art*, 8 (Spring 1951), pp. 110-111. Moe Reinblatt had been Bercovitch's student, close friend, and admirer from 1934, when he enrolled in Bercovitch's class at the YWHA in Montreal, until Bercovitch died in 1951. Reinblatt made it clear that the association with Bakst was Bercovitch's proudest memory. Jack Gordon, Bercovitch's student from 1938 to 1940, confirmed this in a Montreal interview, 27 November 1986, as did Eudice Garmaise, Bercovitch's student from 1935 to 1939, interviewed

in Montreal, 10 December 1986. In 1926, Bercovitch spoke specifically of his experience at the school with Dobujinsky to Sophie Heyden, interviewed in Montreal, 1 June 1987.

20. Artist's information to Canadian National Gallery Archives, 16 June 1942.

21. Frank Whitford, *Kandinsky* (N.Y.: Hamlyn, 1967), p. 10.

22. Hamilton, *Pelican History of Art,* p. 182.

23. Baila V'Dovetz interview, August 1977.

24. Ibid.

25. Ibid.

26. Ibid.

27. For an excellent history of the early Habima Theatre, see Raikin Ben-Ari, *Habima* (N.Y.: Yoseloff, 1957).

28. V.E. Barnett, *Kandinsky at the Guggenheim* (N.Y.: Abbeville Press, 1983), pp. 297-9. In 1917 the NKP (People's Commissariat for Enlightenment) was established under Anatoly Lunacharsky. In 1918 the IZO (Department of Visual Arts) was established within the NKP. In July 1918 Kandinsky became director of the theatre and film sections of IZO-NKP.

29. Ben-Ari, *Habima,* p. 202. The version by Gozzi should not be confused with Puccini's 1926 opera. The Chinese fable had many interpreters.

30. Long after Bercovitch left Russia in 1926, he was to meet again one of his colleagues from the Habima period. The Habima actress, Chayele Grober (Ben-Ari, *Habima*, pp. 29, 156), was by 1940 in Montreal and directing the Yiddish Theatre Group. For its dramatization of one of J.I. Segal's poems, she engaged as set designer her old friend Bercovitch. I am grateful to Mr. Abe Bogen who drew my attention to Chayele Grober's description of the event in her autobiography *Mein Weg Alein* (Tel Aviv : Perez, 1968), pp. 104-5.

31. Stanislavsky, Meyerhold, and Vachtangov were the three dominant figures of the Moscow theatre at that time. Stanislavsky had taught the other two, but Vachtangov had moved from quiet realism to a more melodramatic approach. Meyerhold had gone much further, to extreme stylization and non-realism.

32. Divorce in immediately post-Revolution years in Russia was often no more than a unilateral declaration before a local official who often did not bother to register the declaration. Whatever the law said, there is abundant eye-witness testimony to the practice, including that of the artist's later son-in-law, Solomon Ary (interviewed by the author in Montreal in a series of conversations January - August, 1987). The exact date of Bercovitch's divorce is therefore unknown, but it had certainly been effected by 17 September 1921, at which time Bercovitch made a formal declaration to the Leningrad Academy of Fine Arts that he was single. (Information in a letter dated 18 June 1987 to the author from Mme. Androussenko of the Soviet Academy of Arts and Science.)

33. In the early 1920's the U.S.A. was beginning to restrict immigration, but there is no reason to suppose that Canada was the Avruticks' second choice. See Howe, *Land of our Fathers*, p. 33, where the record shows that, as early as 1900, a group of Jews, intending to emigrate and marching to Hamburg together to escape the anti-semitic mob, had composed a marching song,

"Geyt, yidelech, in der vayter velt ;
  In kanade vet ir ferdinen gelt."
("Go, little Jews, into the wide world ; in Canada you will make a living.")

34. Barnett, *Kandinsky,* pp. 298-9. Kandinsky had founded the first "Inkhuk" (Institute of Artistic Culture) in 1920, and then co-founded, in 1921 with Petr Kogan, the RAKhN (the Russian Academy of Artistic Sciences). One of the responsibilities of this body was the establishment of the new art schools.

35. The Leningrad Academy of Fine Arts has three documents relating to Bercovitch in its archives :

a. his request of 10 October 1921 to be registered by the state as a set-decorator.

b. an accompanying document, dated 17 September 1921, in which Bercovitch declares himself single, a set-decorator by profession, born 15 March 1891 at Kherson, and living in Petrograd (Leningrad). [This last item was not strictly true : he was still in Moscow. He was evidently anticipating acceptance at the Stigliz Academy.]

c. a 1922 admission certificate to the Stigliz Academy in Leningrad.

The above information is contained in a letter dated 18 June 1987 to the author from Mme. Androussenko of the Foreign Relations Department of the Soviet Academy of Arts and Science. Mme. Androussenko points out that Bercovitch was registered at the Stigliz Academy for the academic year beginning 1922, but not for the following year. She mentions the possibility that his lack of an orthodox "formation de base" might have been the cause of his leaving the Stigliz before it became part of the Leningrad Academy proper in 1923. This hypothesis, however, does not take into account the attractiveness of the 1922 opportunity to teach and paint in Ashkabad.

36. See information supplied by Bercovitch to the Canadian National Gallery Archives 9 May 1932, and 16 June 1942. See also "The Development of Painting in Canada," *National Gallery of Canada 1945 Exhibition Catalogue* (Toronto : Ryerson, 1945), p. 51.

37. Mme. Androussenko of the Soviet Academy in letter to author, 18 June 1987.

Plate 1.
Private collection

"A Moscow Face" 1922
pencil on paper
33 x 25 cm.

Top left — A detail from Bercovitch's 1920 painting of Kalmushe, his son by his first wife.

Top right — Kalmushe and his mother, Baila, in Palestine, c. 1941.

Bottom left — Kalmushe (Kalman Barkov, as he became in Israel) at 29, shortly before his accidental death on August 19, 1949.

Photos from Kalman Barkov memorial book. (Author's files)

CHAPTER TWO

Ashkabad

Turkestan is the vast area stretching between Siberia to the north and Iran and Afghanistan to the south. Marco Polo's Golden Road had led through Turkestan: its cities, Samarkand, Tashkent, Alma-Ata, Bokhara, and Ashkabad, were part of legend.

Ashkabad, when Bercovitch arrived in 1922, was a city of more than thirty thousand souls.[1] To its north was the great Kara Kum Desert: behind the city to the south were the foothills of the mountains of Iran. Irrigation made crops possible, and there was some sparse grazing for sheep and Turkoman horses, but life was sustained only as a result of great care and effort.

The Revolution had not come easily. Immediately after the events of October 1917, Moslem leaders in Turkestan took advantage of the confusion to proclaim independent Islamic states. These were short-lived, however, and power was seized by the Bolsheviks in early 1918, but they in turn were defeated within months by pro-Tsarist forces. It was not until March 1921 that the Bolsheviks obtained a final and decisive victory over both the White armies and the Moslem followers of the Amir of Bokhara. The All-Russian Central Executive Committee then formally established Turkestan as an autonomous republic, but guerilla warfare by both counter-revolutionary and Moslem factions continued for some years, and Ashkabad became a centre of conspiracy and assassination.[2]

When Bercovitch arrived in this exotic but disturbed environment in the fall of 1922, he made a startling discovery. The school at which he was to teach existed only on paper. The unsettled conditions had delayed its physical establishment, and the necessary funds had not yet arrived from the central authorities. The thirty-one year old artist faced the very real possibility of starvation.

Help arrived, however, and from a very unexpected quarter. Bercovitch received a letter from Bryna, still in Moscow and still pregnant. She wrote to say that she had moved to a room on the seventh floor of a tenement building and that she never wanted to see him again. A return address was written clearly on both the letter and the envelope.

Bercovitch replied immediately. He was starving, he told her, and she was to send such money or food as the parcels from Montreal would provide or he would throw himself into the nearest river.

Bryna sent help, although it is not clear as to whether or not she realised at the time how empty was the threat, since Ashkabad was far indeed from water of any kind. (Later, in Montreal, the melodrama of Bercovitch's plea would be remembered and would become the basis of a family joke, as in Bryna's occasional shopping instruction to her children, "if you do not go and buy a bottle of milk, I shall throw myself under a streetcar.") She stayed in Moscow but began to subsidise Bercovitch modestly but regularly out of the gifts from her three brothers in Montreal, and the correspondence between Bercovitch and herself became increasingly affectionate. She was able to spare the help even after the birth of her daughter on April 15, 1923, because she had found work in a state-run nursery. Moscow was crowded with emaciated orphaned or abandoned children, pitiful victims of the Civil War or of the

Plate 2.
From the collection of
Beatrice & Bernard Bazar

"Head of a Woman — Ashkabad" c. 1923
oil on burlap
36 x 25 cm.

Plate 3.
From the collection of
Colman and Sandor Klein

"Three Horsemen" c. 1923
tempera on paper
75 x 71 cm.

23

famines, and Bryna was employed as a wet-nurse. As she said later, "they stuck to my breast like spiders." Her daughter, Sara, born plump and healthy, was the star of the nursery. She was trotted out for all the visitors from the Western countries as a shining example of the success of Soviet child-rearing methods. The truth was that only the Montreal connection made life possible for Bryna and her child. When one parcel failed to arrive on time and she had to sell her winter coat to buy food, Bryna realised how precarious was her situation. When a letter arrived from Bercovitch with news of the school established and a regular salary, she accepted his offer of reconciliation and a fresh start and took the train for Ashkabad.

Bercovitch left his cramped and sparsely furnished bachelor room, and the couple rented a two-storey house, a low white building with a pleasantly shaded courtyard behind. They acquired a cat, "Mirutschka", and a dog, "Boxer", and settled into what seemed very like domestic bliss. Sara's earliest memories are of contentment, riding on the milk-man's donkey as her father held her, the milk-cans clattering all around her, or on her father's back, looking down at the red and green flowers embroidered into his Turkoman cap. At five feet eleven inches, Bercovitch was taller than most Turkomen, and his daughter felt that she was part of an imposing spectacle as she rode on her father's shoulders down the dusty streets of Ashkabad.

After the school opened, and after Bryna arrived, Bercovitch began to react enthusiastically to his surroundings. On salary, at peace with his wife, and free from the fear of hunger, he could permit himself to respond freely to his new environment and he threw himself into his painting with renewed fervour.

One aspect of his work never changed, the interest in portraiture that he had always had and that he would retain for the rest of his life. In his "Head of a Woman — Ashkabad" (oil c. 1923 — see Plate 2), there is the same strong line as in an earlier and less complex work, "A Moscow Face" (pencil 1922 — see Plate 1), and the same clarity of intention. In "Head of a Woman — Ashkabad", Bercovitch builds the face with a divided brush stroke, ochre upon ochre, the whole profile outlined with a strong dark brown line that permits no distraction. It is a strong peasant face, and Bercovitch's treatment is very modern in its simplicity. The background and the woman's hair are so similar in rich texture as to be almost one, and the effect is to focus attention even more on the strength of the face. Further, by cropping the head and by having the subject stare out beyond the painting into a distance perceived only by herself, Bercovitch creates a compelling study of character.

At the same time, Bercovitch was becoming increasingly affected by the colours and folk-art of Turkestan. They would come to influence his work as profoundly as the art forms of Morocco had influenced Matisse ten years earlier. Folk-art in itself was not, of course, a new experience for Bercovitch. His earliest training had been in the painting of ikons, certainly in Russia the purest and most complete manifestation of folk-culture. He had also been aware, in the Odessa days with David Burliuk, of the interest Burliuk and Natalia Goncharova were taking, not only in ikons, but in such esoteric art-forms as Siberian embroidery.[3] It was also not Bercovitch's first exposure to Islamic decorative art: he had seen much in Jerusalem. The new experience lay in his awareness of the abundance and complexity of Turkoman carpet design, and of the power of the Turkestan landscape.

He began to experiment with his own carpet designs, and often incorporated the patterns into his painting. The sharp angles and geometric shapes of "Three Horsemen" (tempera c. 1923 — see Plate 3) owe as much to Bercovitch's studies of Turkoman carpets as they do to his understanding of Cézanne.

In "Three Horsemen", Bercovitch, with an expressive integrity honed in Munich, demonstrates the freshness and wonder of his own perception of Turkomen in their element. The three riders fill the landscape. Immensely skilled, they revel in the perfection of their horsemanship. The subject is one of folk-art, but the treatment is one of great sophistication. The tall woollen hats, emblems of the riders' ethnic identity, are rendered absolutely faithfully, while the riders themselves are drawn in modern simplicity in the same colours as the background, from which they are separated only by thin outlines. Man is both dominant and individual and yet at one with Nature. Nature itself is animated by colours that are expressive entities in their own right. Rhythmically angular mountains jut into a sky whose green never existed but as a function of the artist's perception. Fixed for eternity, the horsemen yet embody power and movement. By cropping the third rider, and indeed realizing him less completely than the other two, Bercovitch suggests not only the energy of the subjects but the dynamism of his own creative process. The third rider is in the process of coming into being.

The insistent, repeated angular patterns have a simple intensity which combines with the expressive use of colour to produce a totally satisfying harmony of colour, line, and subject.

Bercovitch's experiment with complete freedom in the use of colour is vividly illustrated in "Two Turkestan Women" (oil c. 1924 — see Plate 7). The furious red of the sky, executed with heavy impasto, is not an external phenomenon, but rather the inner impression of the artist, and the result is the creation of a passionate oneness between man and his universe. The oneness is intensified by the use of the same powerful red for the two women, prominent figures separated from the sky only by the heavy black of their outlines. The green of the foreground is one never seen in Nature, but it forms an effective and refreshing contrast with the dominant red. The cropping of the figures is a preferred device of Bercovitch in this period, creating as it does a sense of immediacy and eliminating any distance between the viewer and the object.

"The Balalaika Player" (tempera 1924 — see Plate 6) is more closely akin to "Three Horsemen" than to "Two Turkestan Women". Here the artist's interest is primarily in pattern as a vehicle of mood. The face of the balalaika player, like the moustaches and eyebrows of the spectators, is composed of geometric shapes as regular as those of any carpet design. The painting is at the same time an exercise in ochres, indicating a mood rather than an attempt to present reality. The figures are in a circle, accentuating a harmony and rhythm already created by colour and the repetition of familiar shapes. The three women, although separated physically from the men, are thus united with them by the artist's treatment.

In the same year, 1924, Bercovitch painted the large "Three Turkomen Drinking Tea" (tempera 1924 — see Plate 5), in which he permitted the material, in this case brown paper, to show much more clearly than was usual in his work. It takes on a value other than that of mere medium. This is particularly evident in the treatment of the tall woollen hat and the robe of the central figure. Both are no more than divided brush-strokes of single colour, black for the hat and red or brown for the robe, imposed on still-visible brown paper, but the effect is one of simplicity, boldness of line, and strength. There is strength too, even brutality, in the men's faces, each no more than a few confident lines, but the whole effect is made gentle by the soft patterns of the foreground. These are rendered in a surprisingly painterly way, unlike the strong, geometric patterns of the background. The control of both pattern and colour is exquisitely delicate. The green of the teacup on the floor is picked up, not only in the two held teacups, but in the background pattern behind the main figure. Thus the gentleness of the tea ceremony

and the opposing masculinity of the three subjects are brilliantly reconciled by pattern and colour.

Bercovitch was so joyful in his creativity that he was able to take almost in his stride Bryna's news in the spring of 1925 that she was once again pregnant. Sara was forever touching his beloved art books and magazines, so difficult to obtain in Ashkabad, and two children were likely to be more of a nuisance than one, but everything else at the moment was going so well. He was happy with his painting and Bryna was gainfully employed in work that interested her. Their home was comfortable, his teaching presented no problem, and he was enjoying a sustained financial security that he had never previously attained. In the circumstances he was prepared to be magnanimous, and there was no argument about the coming birth.

Bryna had not been idle while Bercovitch taught and painted. Ashkabad, like the Moscow she had left, was full of homeless children, victims of the Revolution, of civil war, and of famine. As she put it herself, "in the year 1924, Tashkent, Samarkand, Ashkabad, and other cities of the Soviet Orient were flooded with thousands and thousands of homeless boys. Like beasts they would descend on a city and terrorize the whole population." (For a full account of the problem and how Bryna and her comrades dealt with it, see Appendix 3.) It was a challenge that Bryna Avrutick could not resist, and she threw herself wholeheartedly into the setting up of a school and living-quarters for these orphans.

Once the "colony for the homeless" had been established, and its clientele persuaded to enter it, Bryna began to receive a small salary as a teacher. The income was precious to Bryna in that it gave her a measure of economic independence, and was more than enough to pay for a housekeeper to look after her daughter.

There was nothing to distract Bercovitch from his work, no domestic problem and no financial worry. Every walk he took provided him with a new subject. He continued to be fascinated by the strength of the Turkoman face. One such study is that of "Two Turkomen" (oil c. 1925 — see Plate 8). With its cropped heads and lack of foreground and background, it has the same sense of capturing the immediate and the instant as does a photograph. One face, full of strength and powerful planes of colour, is juxtaposed with another, weaker and delineated with a shorter, less assured brushstroke. It is a striking study of a relationship caught in the moment and laid bare.

And there was always the wonder of the Ashkabad landscape to record. In "Ashkabad: Low Building and Blue Mountains" (oil 1924 — see Plate 4), the

Plate 4.
From the collection of
Clare & Charles Schulman

"Ashkabad — Low Building & Blue Mountains" 1924
oil on board
41 x 52 cm.

Plate 5.
From the collection of
Blanche & Honoré Parent

"Three Turkomen Drinking Tea" 1924
tempera on paper
110 x 75 cm.

viewer is drawn into a passionate, turbulent Nature. The diagonal brushstroke of the foreground leads the eye first to the vertical middleground, with its pure planes of ochre and cream, and then to the horizontal and marvellous motion of the mountains and the sky. Forms are powerful and simplified and colour is dramatic and unreal. The large swirling strokes of the mountains and the sky create a vibrant and exciting Nature. The influence of Van Gogh is apparent. The universe is in motion and the artist is responding with the intensity and the integrity of his whole being.

The situation, perfect in every respect, was too good to last, and problems began for Bercovitch and Bryna Avrutick even before the birth of their second child. The scheme with which Bryna was involved, to house and train homeless boys, ran into difficulties. Government money and supplies, vital to the programme, were often delayed, and there were shortages of food. The boys, always reluctant participants, reverted easily to their old habits of violence and brigandage. The "colony" slowly disintegrated; the staff was released; and Bryna was faced with a loss of both income and, temporarily, a sense of purpose in her daily life. Her faith in the ultimate rightness of her cause was undiminished, however, and her new daughter, born on September 3, 1925, was called Ninel, an anagram of Lenin. No doubt, in time, Bryna would have found another outlet for her revolutionary fervour, but misfortune overcame her and Bercovitch before that could happen.

What would turn into a major disaster began very innocently. Bercovitch, who liked to tell stories in spite of his stammer, decided one night to regale Bryna and their friends with tales of intrigue. He had discovered that the school at which he taught was a centre of White Russian conspiracy. Without any political commitment himself, he found nothing but amusement in the whispered conversations of his colleagues, full of codewords and nostalgia. Bercovitch and the guests were amused: Bryna was horrified. Without consulting Bercovitch, she hurried to the Education Commissariat and denounced the school as a nest of counter-revolutionaries. What she did not know, and found out only later, was that the personnel of the Commissariat were involved in the plotting. Within weeks, Bercovitch was summarily dismissed, without explanation.

It was only then that Bryna realised that her only evidence was hearsay, that Ashkabad was a long way from Moscow, and that there was in fact no one to whom they could appeal. They were unemployed and without even the possibility of earning an income. They also had two young children and were living in a famine area. As their situation grew desperate, Bryna wrote to her brothers in Montreal.

The reply was immediate and took the form of a steamship ticket for the family and sufficient funds to cover their travelling expenses. The Avrutick brothers had never been happy with their sister in as alien an environment as Turkestan, and had often suggested that she, Bercovitch, and the children join them in Canada. Yankel, the oldest brother, whose wife had recently died, offered his sister and Bercovitch a home with him until they were able to establish themselves. There was one small technicality: Bryna and Bercovitch were not married, and Canada was not likely to accept an unmarried couple, especially one with two children. Bryna was opposed to the institution of marriage, but there was no alternative. In the first week of May 1926, Bryna Avrutick became Bryna Bercovitch, and on May 9 Bercovitch obtained a Russian passport. (See Appendix 4. It is clear that neither Bercovitch nor Bryna dismissed the possibility of returning to their native Russia at a later date. In Bryna's case she spoke of returning after doing some propaganda work in Canada. They both expected a better Russian society to emerge after the initial post-Revolution difficulties and after Socialist planning had had time to eradicate famine. Bercovitch's 1926 Russian passport was valid for only one year and it is significant that he went to the trouble of renewing it in Montreal in 1927. It was never used.)

The two adults and the two children were to leave from Riga. Riga and Hamburg were the two most frequently used ports of embarkation by Eastern European emigrants, and the Montreal brothers had made a Riga — London — Montreal booking for their sister and her family. The train ride from Ashkabad to Riga was a long one, of many days, with a multitude of stops and changes. Travel under such circumstances, with two small children, was tiring, and Bercovitch and Bryna decided to break the journey in Moscow. They stayed for a few days with friends from the Habima days. Moscow was as exciting as ever, and Bercovitch was tempted.

"You go," he said to his wife, "and I'll follow later."

Bryna knew that, if she agreed, she and the children would never see him again. She insisted that the family stay together.

On June 1, 1926, Alexander and Bryna Bercovitch, together with their daughters Sara and Ninel, left Riga. They were bound for Montreal and a new life.

---

1. "Turkestan," *Encyclopaedia Britannica*, 1926.

2. Ibid. Enver Pasha was assassinated as late as August 1923.

3. Gray, *The Great Experiment*, p. 87.

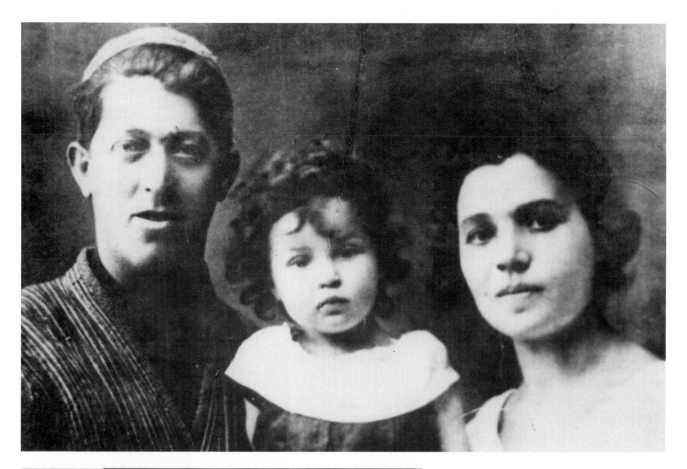

Top — 1925 in Ashkabad. Bryna and Bercovitch with their two year-old daughter, Sara. Bercovitch is wearing Turkoman dress. Bryna's dark beauty makes it clear why Bercovitch called her "my Gauguin woman".

Bottom — June 1926. Bercovitch's photograph of his family on the ship that is taking them from Riga to Montreal. Bercovitch is now 36 and Bryna 31. Sara (Sylvia, as she will be known in Montreal) is 3, and Ninel is ten months.

Photos : author's files

Plate 6.
From the collection of
Blanche & Honoré Parent

"Balalaika Player" 1924
tempera on paper
26 x 35 cm

Plate 7.
Private collection

"Two Turkestan Women" c. 1924
oil on cardboard
17 x 26 cm.

CHAPTER THREE

Montreal: 1926

Alexander Bercovitch and his family landed in Montreal on June 20, 1926, and began, as arranged, to share the home of the blacksmith Yankel Avrutick and his seven children.

They entered a crowded little world, an almost completely self-contained Yiddish-speaking community in the middle of a North American city. In a sprawling Montreal of one million people, most of the fifty thousand Jewish inhabitants[1] lived in a clearly defined area of about two square kilometers at the eastern foot of Mount Royal, the hill and natural park that dominates the city (see map — page 36). The Jewish community straddled St. Lawrence Boulevard, Montreal's principal north-south thoroughfare. To the west lived the Protestant English minority, the economic ascendancy; to the east lived the French.[2]

Most buildings in the central city area, other than stores or tenement buildings, were triplexes, peculiarly Montreal structures of three dwellings perched one on top of the other. Access to the higher units was, and is, by outside wrought-iron or wooden staircases. A typical city block would consist of attached and uninterrupted triplexes, and each third of a triplex would usually house three generations of a family. Many would take in one or two boarders — relatives or friends — and the houses overflowed with people.

This spirit of moral obligation on the part of the rich to help the poor was inherent in the life of Jewry in Europe... Families of better means aided their less fortunate brethren; immigrants pooled their resources. Sharing was the accepted thing. Families planned and economized to the point of self-sacrifice in order to help each other out... they housed their fellow 'landsleit' and they boarded their friends. They did so with a free mind, with hopefulness born of anticipation of better days.[3]

Most immigrants worked in factories, in sweatshop conditions, and for low wages, and the contribution of the boarders to the household budget was essential. There were always more relatives to be sent for, more steamship tickets to be bought. Whole families were brought, one member at a time, out of the misery of Eastern Europe. Some immigrants, through sacrifice, were able to open small businesses, though entrepreneurial freedom meant eighty or ninety hour work weeks. Nevertheless, some prospered and went on to be the patriarchs and matriarchs of great business dynasties. Others foundered. Most merely survived, only just able to meet the weekly bills. Life was, however, informed by hope, and it was lived intensely.

Of one thing these immigrants were certain. They were facing rare and golden opportunities of a new world being discovered and constructed. In that world they — or their children — would succeed.[4]

Plate 8.
Private collection

"Two Turkomen" c. 1925
oil on board
41 x 33 cm.

34

Plate 9.
From the collection of
Malca Friedman

"Bare Trees and Fir Trees" c. 1929
oil on cardboard
16 x 21 cm.

Montreal in 1926

By 1926, most Jewish immigrants lived in an area twelve blocks long and twelve blocks wide. It was bounded by Bernard Avenue to the north, Park Avenue to the west, Drolet Street to the east, and Sherbrooke Street to the south. It was bisected by Montreal's principal north-south artery, St. Lawrence Boulevard, known to Montrealers as "the Main". The densely populated ghetto area lay at the eastern foot of Mount Royal, and "the mountain", as it was always called, was the community's playground. This was especially true of that slice of the park called Fletcher's Field, which was immediately adjacent to the immigrant area.

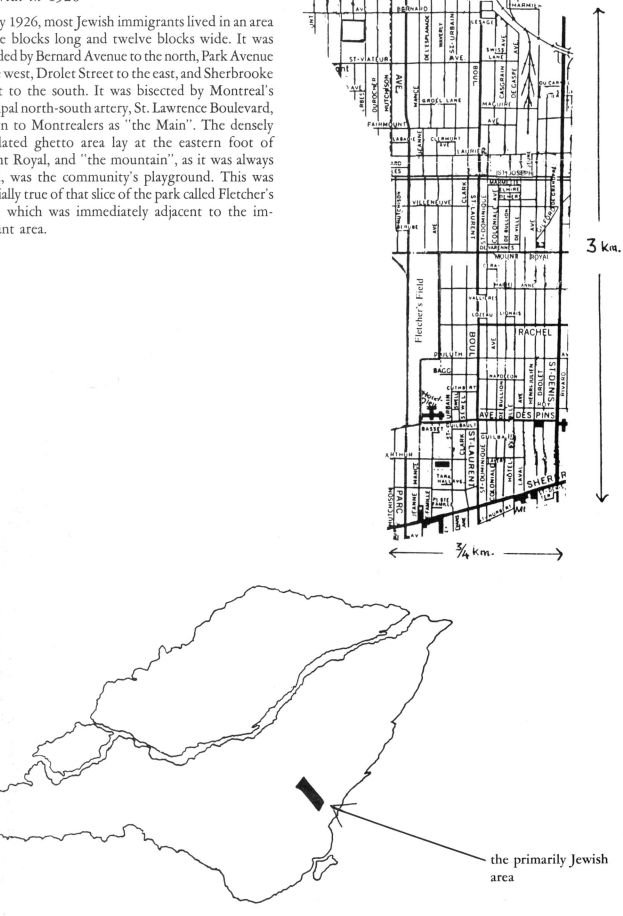

the primarily Jewish area

Every immigrant was willing to work towards a better world, but there was little agreement as to how that better world might be achieved or as to what form it would take. Each shade of political or religious opinion formed an association, from the Zionist Society and the Hadassah,[5] to the Arbeiter Ring (Workmen's Circle),[6] or the Communist Party, with its busy headquarters at 62 Rachel Street East.[7] Union activity was constant, and there were endless meetings.[8] The young had a similar richness of choice, from the Zionist Farband to YPSL (The Young People's Socialist League) or the YCL (Young Communist League), and parents could find a school for their offspring that would match exactly their own ideological outlook. For the religiously inclined there were the Talmud Torah schools, and for the secular left there was the Arbeiter Ring Shule. The Peretz Shule and the Folk Shule provided alternatives for those whose views lay somewhere between the two extremes. (A child attending one of these private community schools did so after completing a full day's study at the Protestant public school.[9] The child of a Jewish immigrant had a much longer school day than his English or French counterpart.) The community was full of strong and differing opinions, and there were two Jewish newspapers in which to take issue with the opposition. (The same St. Lawrence Boulevard company published both the Yiddish *Der Kanader Adler* — The Canadian Eagle — and the English-language *Canadian Jewish Chronicle*.)[10]

Yet, in spite of constant and noisy argument, there was massive non-sectarian mutual assistance. There were so many philanthropic and self-help societies that, in 1917, it was necessary to bring them together under one umbrella organization, the Federation of Jewish Philanthropies.[11]

All this activity was generated by a population no more than five per cent of Montreal's total, crammed into an area only twelve city blocks square.

The cultural life of the community was no less frenzied. The Jewish Public Library made its basement hall available for any kind of creative activity, and itself invited an impressive list of visiting speakers, from Sholem Aleichem on.[12] For the theatre-goer there was always a visiting company from New York's Yiddish theatre at the Monument National on St. Lawrence.[13] Jewish Montrealers were richer by far in theatre opportunity than their English or French neighbours.[14] The community's amateur and semi-professional groups ranged from the English-language productions of the ''Y''[15] to the Yiddish ''Arteg'' (Jewish Workers' Theatre Group) or Sigmund Lev's ''Thealig'' (under the auspices of

the Jewish National Workers' Alliance).[16] Acronyms abounded, and every club had a drama group.

It was summer when Bercovitch arrived in the ghetto, and families spilled out of the overcrowded homes on to the sidewalks. Women called out to each other from their balconies, and shoppers and gossipers filled the stores and the markets. Peddlers and fruit-sellers and icemen cried their wares and bargained with the mothers, careful with their pennies. The grassless streets bulged with horses and wagons and trucks and streetcars and racing, shrieking children and the whole noise of humanity at work and play. Only on Saturdays did mothers put families into their finery to take the fresh air on the promenade at the foot of Fletcher's Field.

In the evenings, after the long day at work and after the meetings, cafés were popular. The most frequented was Horn's, and there was urgent competition for the tables near the big windows and the passing strollers on St. Lawrence Boulevard, but the politically committed occupied the long tables further inside. Ten cents for a coffee and a Danish pastry bought an evening's right to a wrought-iron chair and hours of argument. (Fortunately for Horn's, there was a lucrative lunchtime trade serving the workers of the area, including the staff of the nearby *Kanader Adler* and *Chronicle*.)[17]

To Bercovitch, fresh from four years of tranquillity, space, and beauty in Ashkabad, the frenetic life of the ghetto, and Yankel Avrutick's suffocatingly small house on City Hall Street,[18] must have seemed like bedlam. There was no time, however, for regrets or recrimination: there were twelve people in the household and Yankel Avrutick alone could not carry the economic burden. Bercovitch had to find work.

Within a week of stepping off the boat he had his first job. Bryna's brother Nachman, the teacher of Yiddish, had married into the Lipes family, and a cousin, Sam Lipes, who owned a wholesale fruit company, offered Bercovitch his first Canadian commission. On a huge grimy wall, opposite the railway freight sheds on Rolland Street, Bercovitch was to paint the legend ''Lipes Fruit'' and a picture of a boy holding a bunch of grapes. The experience can only have been dispiriting, but it gave Bercovitch a new Canadian friend, the fruit company's office manager, Louis Muhlstock.[19] Muhlstock, who had been brought by his family from Galicia to Canada at the age of seven, was an artist who had already exhibited at the 1925 Spring Show of the Art Association of Montreal (later the Montreal Museum of Fine Arts).[20] He was attending the life classes in the studio above the Art Association two evenings a week, and had just enrolled at the Ecole des Beaux-

Plate 10.
Private collection

"Coloniale Avenue" 1932
oil on board
50 x 46 cm.

Plate 11.
From the collection of
Harold B. Gordon

"Harbour Scene" c. 1938
gouache & pastel on paper
42 x 60 cm.

Arts[21] for a further two evenings. Although Muhlstock was saving desperately to be able to study in Paris,[22] he nonetheless invited Bercovitch to join him at the life classes as his guest. Bercovitch, who could afford neither materials nor model, leaped at the chance. This was his second venture into the Montreal art world.

The first had been effected even before the meeting with Louis Muhlstock. While exploring St. Lawrence, Bercovitch had seen oil paintings in a store window and had gone in to enquire about their origin. The ensuing conversation with the proprietor marked the beginning of a twenty-five year friendship. The store belonged to Bernard Mayman, who had been born in Poland and who had studied art in England at the Royal Academy before coming to Canada in 1912. After finding it impossible to make a living from his art, he had opened a sign-painting business and had just moved to St. Lawrence from nearby Drolet Street when Bercovitch walked into his store, attracted by the display of Mayman's unsold canvases. Mayman still painted in every spare moment and encouraged artists to use his store as a meeting-place. He made paint and materials available to them at wholesale prices, and there was always a basket of fruit near the chairs he put out for his friends. Sixty years later, Mayman's daughter, Sophie Mayman Heyden, still remembers that June day in 1926 when a burly stranger with a hesitant manner came into the store to ask who had painted the canvases in the window. She was seventeen at the time and working for her father. Her first job every morning was to buy fruit at nearby Rachel Street Market for the basket in the store.[23] Over the years, the circle that met at Mayman's would include Bercovitch, Joe Sher, Jack Beder, Harry Mayerovitch, Regina Seiden (until her marriage to Eric Goldberg), Charles and Marguerite Fainmel, Louis Muhlstock, Sam Borenstein, and Frank Iacurto.

It was from Mayman and Muhlstock that Bercovitch learned how desolate was the Montreal art scene. As Muhlstock puts it:

> Montreal was raw. We had one museum, the Art Association of Montreal. There was no Picasso, no Chagall, no Modigliani, no Léger, there was nothing. We had paintings of the Dutch school, of the nineteenth century, that kind of painting. There were only two galleries in Montreal, the Watson Gallery on Sherbrooke Street, and the Johnson Gallery on Ste. Catherine Street. There were no places for young people with no reputation as yet to ex-

hibit... The Watson Gallery showed the work of Academicians and of the Dutch painters.[24]

(There were in fact two more galleries in 1926 than Muhlstock remembers, that of W. Scott & Sons, and the Sidney Carter Studio, though Carter was primarily a photographer and art sales were initially a sideline.)

There was no opportunity to study any of the developments in art in the twentieth century. The life classes at the Art Association were organized by the Royal Canadian Academy, which was "a private club of wealthy English-speakers who still preferred the late nineteenth century Dutch artists."[25] The Ecole des Beaux-Arts, founded three years earlier, was no real alternative. It was a stronghold of conservatism, steadfastly opposed to the kind of excitement and Expressionist intensity that informed Bercovitch's work.[26] The Ecole des Beaux-Arts also limited its exhibitions to work by its own past and present students, thus denying itself access to the little nourishment that the rest of the Montreal art world might have afforded it.

The few commercial galleries showed what the Montreal public wanted, the works of the traditional masters for those who could pay for them, and reproductions of the same works for those who couldn't.[27] The Art Association itself would buy no contemporary art before 1939.[28] Montreal in 1926 was what it would still be in 1939 when Robert Ayre called it "the last pasture of the contented Dutch cow."[29]

Art and artists seemed to be faring better in Toronto. The Group of Seven, with its first exhibition in 1920, had tried to revitalize Canadian art "through the continued exploration and interpretation of the Canadian landscape,"[30] but this movement offered little appeal to those of European background with an interest in Man or Man's works. There was, in any event, little Toronto-Montreal cross-fertilization,[31] and there is evidence that, by the late 1920's, a certain rigidity had set in even among the Group of Seven. The revolution, the use of landscape as identity, had become institutionalized, some alleged, and the "fashionable folk-art" repetitive.[32] It is clear that the Toronto-based Group, together with its short-lived Montreal affiliate, the Beaver Hall Group (1920-21),[33] had little in common with the internationalism of painters like Bercovitch.

Much more important than the influence of the Group of Seven, as far as Bercovitch and the other Montreal artists were concerned, was the power wielded by the artists Alphonse Jongers and Edmond Dyonnet.

Bercovitch's backdrop for *Winterset* by
Maxwell Anderson. Produced in 1938 at the Little
Theatre of the Y in Montreal, it starred Sally Allister
as Miriamne and Howard Schwartz as Mio.

Photo: courtesy of Sally Allister

Plate 12.
From the collection of
Colman and Sandor Klein

"Mr. & Mrs. A.M. Klein" 1934
oil on goldleaf
100 x 75 cm.

Plate 13.
Private collection

"The Artist's Family" 1934
oil on board
70 x 64 cm.

Apart from the commercial galleries, there were only two exhibition outlets in Montreal, the Spring Show at the Art Association and the Biannual RCA Exhibition in the fall. Both were under the artistic control, direct or otherwise, of Edmond Dyonnet, at the time the secretary of the Academy (a post he was to hold for thirty-two years).[34] An arch-conservative, he was virulently opposed to all modernism, beginning with the Impressionists. It was Dyonnet who later declared, in 1944, that he would never again attend an exhibition which contained "fearful paintings by an insane man" for whom he had "an intense hatred".[35] The "insane man" was Van Gogh.

Jongers, a great friend and supporter of Dyonnet,[36] was the premier portrait painter of Montreal. Into his studio at the Ritz-Carlton Hotel flowed the cream of Montreal society, including two former Governors-General, assorted stockbrokers, and a variety of bankers, all to have their likenesses rendered at $3,000.00 to $5,000.00 a head, the works to be presented at the Spring Show before installation in the appropriate boardroom.[37] Jongers was a very competent craftsman, but he made no serious pretense to innovation or to greatness. To his intimates,

he made the most cynical of remarks, "en Europe j'ai fait de l'art : ici, je fais de l'or."*[38] If the uncritical Anglo-Protestant hierarchy was willing to give, Jongers was willing to receive. Except for a brief exile from the hotel beginning in 1929 because of stock-market reverses, Jongers would continue to live and to paint at the Ritz-Carlton until his death in 1945.

The Dyonnet-Jongers axis dominated the Montreal art world of 1926, and only hindsight permits the onlooker to see glimmers of hope. Alfred Pellan had just won his scholarship to Paris,[39] John Lyman would settle in Montreal in 1931, and Fritz Brandtner would arrive in 1934. The situation would improve, but Bercovitch could not have known that. He was aware only of the sterility of the Montreal art scene and of the famine of opportunity. The portfolio he had brought with him from Russia excited no response in the galleries, and no one knew or cared that he had worked and studied with the great ones. "The immigrants who had the background to understand his work had no money with which to buy it."[40]

---

* "in Europe I made art : here, I make money"

1. Canadian Census figures. The Jewish population of Montreal in 1901 had been a little over 7,000. Most of the Jews of 1926 were, therefore, fairly recent arrivals. Of the original 7,000, many had prospered and had moved to Outremont, a central suburb slightly to the north-west of the original area of settlement. They had their own structures, like the Montefiore Club, founded in 1880, "the dignified retreat of community leaders," see Vladimir Grossman ed., *Canadian Jewish Year Book 1939-40* (Montreal : Woodward, 1939), p. 387. It is worth noting that the Jewish presence in Canada began as early as 1724, with the arrival of Aaron Hart, and that the first synagogue, the Spanish and Portuguese Shearith Israel Congregation, was built in Montreal in 1777. See Arthur D. Hart ed., *The Jew in Canada* (Toronto : Hunter-Rose, 1926), pp. 1, 81.

2. Kathleen Jenkins, *Montreal* (New York : Doubleday, 1966), pp. 465, 515. At the beginning of the century, the Jews of Montreal had been more widely dispersed, as far as Crémazie Boulevard to the north, and Craig Street to the south, but, by 1926, there had been a gradual withdrawal into a smaller and more compact area.

3. Ethel Ostry, "Jewish Social Welfare in Canada," *Canadian Jewish Year Book 1939-40*, p. 103. I am also grateful to my wife, Pearl Brownstein, born on St. Urbain Street in the heart of the ghetto, for first-hand accounts and for many guided tours.

4. Bernard Figler and David Rome, *Hannaniah Meir Caiserman : a Biography* (Montreal : Northern Printing, 1962), p. 32.

5. The Zionist Society (Montreal) was founded in 1898, and the Hadassah (Montreal) in 1916. See Hart ed., *The Jew in Canada*, pp. 74, 277.

6. For a description of the work of the Arbeiter Ring, founded in 1900 and "a beehive for cultural activities", see Myer Fox ed., *Jubilee Book : Thirtieth Anniversary of the Russian Polish Hebrew Sick Benefit Association of Montreal* (Montreal : City Printing Co., 1937), p. 160.

7. For a description of the left-progressive activity of the time, and for an explanation of the choice open to the Jewish adolescent, I am indebted to Ruth Pressman, interviewed 19 May 1987, who arrived in Montreal from her native Kiev in December 1926.

8. The Jewish immigrant community, always feeling itself vulnerable, was anxious to present a united front to the outside world and returned the same city alderman, usually unopposed, throughout the twenties and thirties. First elected in 1922 to represent the St. Louis municipal division, Joseph Shubert had his power base not so much in the Social Democratic Party as in the International Lady Garment Workers' Union. Information given in interview by Ruth and Philip Pressman, Montreal, 5 June 1987. See also Myer Fox ed., *Jubilee Book,* p. 161. (Shubert was not the first Jewish member of the Montreal City Council. Sam Benjamin had been elected to that body in 1849.)

9. All the Jewish schools mentioned were founded between 1898 and 1914. See Hart ed., *The Jew in Canada*, pp. 187-9 for a fuller description of the ideologies they represented. (The Communist Party did not have its own school, the Morris Winchevsky Shule, until the thirties.)

Jews, in 1926, were legally considered Protestants, as opposed to Catholics, and could, if they wished, send their children to the appropriate confessional public school. Jews paid school taxes, but were not permitted to vote for school commissioners until 1973. Within the Protestant public system, Baron Byng High School on St. Urbain Street was effectively a Jewish school from its opening in 1922 until the late 1960's when large scale immigration by new ethnic minorities changed its clientele. (The school finally closed in 1980.) Information confirmed by the Protestant School Board of Greater Montreal, 3 June 1987.

10. The *Canadian Jewish Chronicle* had been founded as the *Canadian Jewish Times* in 1909, changing its name in 1914. The *Canadian Jewish Times* was itself an amalgamation of the *Jewish Times* (founded 1897) and the *Canadian Jewish Tribune* (founded 1908). *Der Kanader Adler,* founded in 1907, was not Montreal's first Yiddish newspaper. *Der Tageblatt* had not survived its first year of publication in 1891. See Hart ed., *The Jew in Canada,* p. 457.

11. The most important of the pre-Federation philanthropic organizations was the Baron de Hirsch Institute, founded in 1890 as the successor to the Young Men's Hebrew Benevolent Society of 1863. Even after 1917, the Baron de Hirsch Institute retained a large measure of autonomy. See Hart ed., *The Jew in Canada,* pp. 71, 197, 201. Among the organizations which did not join the Federation were the fourteen sick benefit societies (the oldest of which was the Hebrew Sick Benefit Society, founded in 1901). See Myer Fox ed., *Jubilee Book,* p. 7.

12. The Jewish Public Library was originally on St. Urbain Street, and was founded in 1914 by Reuben Brainin, the then editor of *Der Kanader Adler,* with only 400 items, mainly brochures and pamphlets. See Grossman ed., *Canadian Jewish Year Book 1939-1940,* p. 308.

13. See Israel Rabinovitch, "Yiddish Theatre in Montreal," *Canadian Jewish Year Book 1940-41,* ed. Vladimir Grossman (Montreal: Woodward, 1940), pp. 161-171, for a full history. By 1926, all efforts to establish a permanent Yiddish theatre in Montreal had failed. The Monument National Theatre, however, provided a temporary home for many visiting New York productions in Yiddish. The first, Jacob Gordin's version of *King Lear,* was in 1898. See Hart ed., *The Jew in Canada,* p. 75.

14. Jenkins, *Montreal,* p. 506. There was no significant French-language theatre before 1940, and Le Théâtre du Nouveau Monde did not open until 1951. His Majesty's Theatre on Guy Street was only one of several theatres available for English-language touring companies, but permanent English theatre began with the Montreal Repertory Theatre in 1930. The Mountain Playhouse followed later in 1952. The National Theatre School (for French and English) opened in 1960, and the theatre and concert complex of the Place des Arts was completed in 1964.

15. The YMHA was founded in 1908 and the YWHA in 1910. The first "Y" dramatic production, *Every-youth,* was staged at the Monument National in 1913. See Sherry Stein ed., *History of the Montreal YM-YWHA 1910-1985* (Montreal: YM-YWHA & NHS Printing, 1985), p. 4.

16. Rabinovitch, "Yiddish Theatre," pp. 169-170.

17. For reminiscences of Horn's, I am obliged, among others, to Jonas London, interviewed at the Elca London Gallery (Montreal) on 22 May 1987, and to Ruth Pressman, interviewed on 19 May 1987.

18. Québec's French Language Law (Bill 101) of 1977 mandates the use of the name "rue de l'hôtel de ville", but, in general, this text will employ the English names of streets and public places in as much as they were the names commonly used by the immigrants of the period.

19. Louis Muhlstock, in an interview on 27 November 1986 at his Ste. Famille Street studio in Montreal.

20. The Montreal Society of Artists was founded in 1847 and changed its name to the Art Association of Montreal in 1860. In 1912 it moved to its present location on Sherbrooke Street, and became the Montreal Museum of Fine Arts in 1949. See the *Official Guide to the Museum, 1977.*

21. The Ecole des Beaux-Arts was founded as "a provincial school offering free tuition" in 1923. See Charles Hill, *Canadian Painting in the Thirties* (Ottawa: National Gallery, 1975), p. 39.

22. Muhlstock left Montreal in 1928 to study in Paris for three years under Louis-François Biloul. He returned to Montreal in 1931 only because of the death of his mother. (Muhlstock interview, 27 November 1986.)

23. Sophie Mayman Heyden, interviewed in Montreal, 1 June 1987.

24. Muhlstock interview 27 November 1986. Later galleries would include the Continental Gallery and Louis Lange's La Galerie de l'Art Français, both opened in 1934, the Dominion Gallery (1940), and the Klinkhoff Gallery (1951). (Dr. Max Stern, who would transform the Canadian art scene after his arrival in Montreal in 1942, was still in his native Düsseldorf: "Dr. Max Stern," *The Gazette* (Montreal), 30 May 1987.)

25. Hill, *Canadian Painting in the Thirties,* p. 39.

26. As late as 1938, the Ecole des Beaux-Arts in Montreal would be attacked as "a centre of cultural fascism and the cause of French-Canadian mediocrity in the arts," Jean-Charles Harvey, "Le pire obstacle à l'art canadien," *Le Jour,* 1, No. 28 (26 March 1938). This was in spite of the influence of Edwin Holgate, who was appointed to teach Graphics after his return from Paris in 1928. The Ecole du Meuble, "the most progressive art school in Montreal" (Hill, *Canadian Art in the Thirties,* p. 117), would not come into being until 1934.

27. In 1949, the professional artists Rita Briansky and Joe Prezament received as a wedding gift from the artists Ghitta Caiserman and Alfred Pinsky a very good reproduction of a Bruegel. That both the givers and the recipients found the gift very appropriate is an indication of the resistance to buying original contemporary art even among artists themselves. Interview with Rita Briansky, Montreal, 29 March 1987.

28. Hill, *Canadian Art in the Thirties,* p. 14.

29. Robert Ayre, " 'Art of Our Day' Attracting Attention by its Vigor in Design," *The Standard* (Montreal), 20 May 1939. Ayre was reviewing the first exhibition by the Contemporary Arts Society.

30. Hill, p. 11.

31. Ibid., p. 42. Charles Hill is quoting Edwin Holgate (in 1973) on how little awareness Montreal artists in the 1920's had of their Toronto counterparts.

32. Inter alia, Bertram Booker, "The Seven Arts," *The Citizen* (Ottawa), 29 December 1928; "their work [that of the Group of Seven] shows signs of hardening into a formula... the 'fashionable' native school of painting."

33. Hill, *Canadian Art in the Thirties,* p. 39. The link between the Group of Seven in Toronto and the Beaver Hall Group in Montreal, notably members Anne Savage and Sarah Robertson, was A.Y. Jackson, who saw their goals as identical. Nevertheless,

Plate 14.
From the collection of
Ricky Dainow

"Path in Park" c. 1934
oil on paper
21 x 31 cm.

Plate 15.
From the collection of
Mrs. Edith Gold and the late Dr. Solomon Gold

"Point-au-Père" c. 1934
oil on board
40 x 55 cm.

as Graham McInnes pointed out, in spite of Jackson's best efforts, "it was not possible that the exuberance of discovery [of the Canadian landscape by the Group of Seven] should wholly appeal to a city and to a people whose tradition in the plastic arts was so strong. Such an approach smacked always in Montreal of a quasi-alien culture," *Canadian Art* (Toronto: McMillan, 1950), p. 72.

34. Colin S. MacDonald ed., *A Dictionary of Canadian Artists* (Ottawa: Canadian Paperbacks, 1967), pp. 185-6. Dyonnet had been Drawing Master at the Council of the Arts (1891-1922), and Professor of Drawing at the Ecole des Beaux-Arts (1923-24), of which he was co-founder.

35. Edmond Dyonnet, *Mémoires d'un Artiste Canadien* (Ottawa: les éditions de l'université d'Ottawa, 1968), p. 91.

36. Ibid., p. 92. When Dyonnet tried, unsuccessfully, to form a new ultra-conservative Society of Canadian Artists in 1944, he proposed as his slate of officers Richard Jack as President, Jongers as Vice-President, and himself as Secretary-Treasurer.

37. See MacDonald ed., *A Dictionary of Canadian Artists,* p. 580. Jongers, born in France in 1872, made his home in Montreal in 1924 (at the Ritz-Carlton Hotel). For a description of the favoured positioning of Jongers' portraits at the Arts Association Spring Shows, I am indebted to Louis Muhlstock, interviewed 27 November 1986.

38. This remark by Jongers was quoted to me on two separate occasions, once by Muhlstock (27 November 1986 interview), and once by Madeleine Boyer, a Montreal model and artist, interviewed in Montreal on 24 January 1987. It was apparently a favourite joke of Jongers and was widely circulated in the artistic community of the time.

39. Hill, *Canadian Art in the Thirties,* p. 119. Alfred Pellan was the first recipient of the Anasthase David Scholarship, the first Québec scholarship to permit the study of art overseas. It was instituted by the same Minister of Education who had set up the Ecoles des Beaux-Arts in Montreal and Québec City. Pellan's return to Québec in 1940 after his success in Paris would provide the long awaited stimulus to artistic development in Québec, particularly among the French-speaking community (Hill, p. 18).

40. Ruth Pressman, interviewed 19 May 1987.

Plate 16.
From the collection of
Harold B. Gordon

''Val Morin — Lake and Trees'' c. 1936
oil on board
50 x 70 cm.

49

CHAPTER FOUR

1927-1933

Adjustment to life in Montreal was proving more difficult than Bercovitch could ever have imagined. His older daughter, Sylvia*, recollects that, in the crowded home of Yankel Avrutick:

> It was very chaotic. My father hated it and my parents quarrelled constantly. My father resented my uncles, all of them.[1]

By the Christmas of 1926, Bercovitch had removed himself and his family from the Avrutick home to a Dorchester Street tenement. Bryna's brothers, concerned about their sister, kept in close touch, and their frequent visits and noisy solicitude enraged Bercovitch. He felt himself overwhelmed by the Avrutick family, and matters came to a head in January 1927.

> It was winter and my uncle Nachman had come to visit. My father picked up a pot from the stove to throw at him. My mother was screaming. I went down from my bed and saw them quarrelling. The door opened and slammed shut. My father left. I didn't see him again for a long time.[2]

After leaving his family, Bercovitch went first to live in a rooming-house at 88 Coloniale Avenue**. It was here that he enjoyed his first artistic success in Canada when one of his watercolours was accepted at the 1927 Spring Show of the Art Association of Montreal. Later in the same year he moved to 2110 Clark Street and there, in the privacy of his rented room, Bercovitch tried to recreate a little corner of Ashkabad. His daughter Sylvia, invited only once to visit, has a memory of the room as a place of colour and wonder, exotic and mysterious. There was a bear-rug on the floor and the smell of incense. On the walls her father had hung not only the paintings he had brought from Turkestan, but also his Turkoman clothes and his guitar. Compared to her own wretched living-quarters, her father's room seemed like Aladdin's cave.

Bryna Bercovitch had been left without any support other than whatever charity the Avruticks might offer. Comrades from the Party urged Bryna to seek a court order for maintenance and, as Sylvia remembers:

> She actually had my father arrested (for which he never forgave her). When the trial came up, the judge asked her if she had told my father to leave. She replied, proudly, 'Yes, of course'. At this, the case was dismissed, and my father was not obligated to give my mother financial support.[3]

(Bryna later told her children that she had thought the Montreal court would be like its Russian counterpart where, as she put it, "women had rights".)

---

* "Sara" had become "Sylvia" as soon as the family arrived in Montreal.

** There is no longer a number as low as 88 on Coloniale Avenue. In 1929 the City Council decided to apply a standard numbering system to all Montreal streets and many addresses changed as a result.

Plate 17.
From the collection of
Judith Borenstein

"Sue Boroff" c. 1935
oil on cloth on board
102 x 59 cm.

52

Plate 18.
Private collection

"Assya" c. 1935
oil on paper on board
34 x 28 cm.

Bryna, who neither wished nor could afford to remain idle, began to teach for her brother Nachman at his Sholem Aleichem Folk Shule. Providing Yiddish and Hebrew instruction to students who had already completed a full day at the public school, it was a shoestring operation which moved from one miserable cold-water flat to another. Whenever space permitted, Bryna and her children would share the premises with the school in order to save on rent. The students' fees were barely enough to meet the school's expenses, including the five dollars a week that made up Bryna's salary, and there was always a fear that parents would find some reason to withdraw their children. At one time, when the "shule" was located on St. Urbain Street, Ninel, the younger daughter, contracted whooping cough. If a coughing fit overtook her during school hours, it was the responsibility of her older sister to lie on top of her in their miniscule bedroom under the stairs and to smother the noise. If word had got out of an infectious disease in the family, it would have resulted in the closing of the school.

All Bryna's non-teaching time was taken up with Party activities. Apart from speaking engagements and from attendance at the frequent mass meetings,[4] she wrote for *Vestnik* (News), a left-wing Russian-language weekly founded in 1928.[5] Except for the Kulturcenter, a "progressive", though not Party-affiliated, literary club,[6] Bryna found the whole social life for herself and her daughters at Party headquarters at 62 Rachel Street East.

> We were taken along to mass meetings, to socials, where there were 'declamations', reciting and singing, as well as some food. I was invariably put on stage to recite poems about the Soviet Army and the capitalist bosses. During the day, when my mother worked, I played in the streets. I can remember coming home from school and being alone, going to the houses of neighbours — poor people with infants crying, dreary rooms with huge old feather beds, the mother cursing the daughter, the children fighting and hurting each other. I don't know what my feelings were at that time. I remember observing these things. No doubt there was an acceptance that that was the way life was. I took care of my little sister, Ninel, pushing her around in a woven wicker carriage. I learned early to keep my complaints to myself. My mother treated me like an adult... The Party slogan

was for children to be independent at a very early age. My mother adhered to this.[7]

Every summer, the Montreal Communist Party organized a camp for children, Camp Neye Velt (New World), at Fourteen Island Lake in the Laurentian Mountains north of Montreal. Bryna worked there for several weeks each year in return for her children's accomodation. The fresh air and freedom of movement were a delight for the girls, although Sylvia remembers that:

> My mother's friends, the 'chavertes' [comrades] of the committee, all big, husky, formidable women, disapproved of me. I was 'wild', they said. I was 'like my father' and would end up 'on the gallows'. But I could feel that somehow my mother liked my wildness.[8]

Bercovitch's contact with his daughters during the years 1927 to 1932 was sporadic, although he spent much of the summer of 1928 near them, working at Camp Nit Gedeiget (Not to Worry), the nearby Party camp for adults. (Among his chores was the painting of the huge sign at the entrance to the camp.)[9]

When he did see the children in Montreal, for the girls it was magic.

> He would appear and take us children out for a couple of hours. He would buy us any toys we wanted, candies, and icecream. He represented the world of fantasy... When he brought me back home, I happily showed my mother the toys he had bought me. She said bitterly, 'Next time tell him to give you bread.' I couldn't see why I should ask for a slice of bread when I could get all those toys instead.[10]

Bercovitch had found a new source of income. Through Bernard Mayman's brother-in-law, Isaac Rosenbloom, he had met George Ganetakos, the founder and general manager of the United Amusement Corporation, and the contractor, Emmanuel Briffa, who decorated the many cinemas and cabarets under Ganetakos' control.[11]

This was the era of exotic interiors in movie palaces, and Briffa was the master of extravagant design and decoration. Cherubs and winged lizards and lightly-clad priestesses cavorted among temples and fountains, and cinemas of the period were fantasies of velvet drapes and chandeliers and starry ceilings. It was Briffa who created the "atmospheres", as he called them, and who realized them in paint and plaster. From the time of his arrival in Montreal in 1910 from his native Malta, Briffa had no serious competition in his field. [12]

He worked not only for the United Amusement Corporation, but for its rival, the Confederation Amusement Corporation, and for churches and synagogues. He assembled a team of craftsmen and together they cut the great stencils, applied the gold and silver leaf, sculpted the bas-reliefs, painted the walls and safety-curtains, and glued the canvases to the ceilings. Joffre Gendron, Briffa's apprentice and successor, now laments:

> People have forgotten how to cut stencils or to apply gold-leaf or to mix paint into plaster to make it look like marble. No one knows how to do that any more. [13]

In 1930, Bercovitch joined the team. It was then made up of the painters David Stark and Walter Shepherd, the designer Jean-Marie "Gene" Hogue, the sculptor and plasterman Joseph Guardo (who later did much work at St. Joseph's Oratory), the gold-leaf specialist Paul Lethiecq, and the apprentice Gendron. [14]

Although every man was a specialist, each could turn his hand to any task, and it is difficult to identify individual work. After nearly sixty years, Gendron can attribute only a few items to Bercovitch with any certainty, and all have been destroyed or covered up. Those in the Montreal area include the underwater scene painted on the lobby walls of the now-closed Snowdon Theatre, the cherubs at the Rialto [15] (photographed by Joffre Gendron before the cinema underwent the remodelling that changed the whole entrance), and the ceiling of Holy Trinity Greek Orthodox Church (burned down in 1985). Briffa himself is known to have signed only one piece, the decorated safety-curtain at Montreal's Rivoli Theatre. [16]

Briffa, Bercovitch, and the others travelled all over Canada, working mainly in the east (although they are known to have decorated the Capitol Theatre in Saskatoon [17]). They lived in hotels, and Gendron remembers that:

> We often moved the furniture aside and prepared the canvases in our rooms. We made such a mess that we would have to repaint the room before we checked out. Bercovitch ate all the time. He got so

heavy that we had to build a special scaffold for him to get up to the ceiling. [18]

Because of his work with Briffa, Bercovitch was, in 1930 and 1931, relatively prosperous. When not away from Montreal, he boarded, sometimes for months at a time, with the family of Berel Silverberg at 3489 St. Lawrence Boulevard, [19] and tried to keep in touch with the immigrant artistic community by dropping in frequently at Mayman's St. Lawrence store. He did little serious painting in the period 1927 to 1932, [20] and when he did it was with the same palette that he had used in Turkestan. "Bare Trees and Fir Trees" (oil c. 1929 — see Plate 9) is very indicative of the state of Bercovitch's mind at the time. The sky is that of Ashkabad, hot, turbulent, and sombre. It is not a Canadian sky but the expression of Bercovitch's frustration. In his mind's eye he still saw Turkestan. He had not yet accepted his new country on its own terms as a stimulus to his creative energy. Mayman's daughter remembers her vivid impression of Bercovitch as he tried to adjust:

> He missed Europe very much. He spoke of little else. This was not his country. He was terribly frustrated. People thought that he was short-tempered, but he was not understood. He was a lonely, broken soul. [21]

One victim of Bercovitch's short temper was Sam Borenstein, the self-taught artist Bercovitch met in 1930 at Cantor's (like Horn's, a popular St. Lawrence Boulevard café). [22] Borenstein had been sculpting since 1928, but gave it up in favour of painting as soon as he saw the work Bercovitch had brought from Turkestan. [23] Borenstein was always grateful to Bercovitch for his initial guidance, in particular for telling him to study the work of Van Gogh, [24] but Bercovitch could be cruel in his criticism. Borenstein's biographers, Kuhns and Rosshandler, write that:

> There was one painter in particular from whom Borenstein desperately wanted criticism — Alexander Bercovitch. One evening he was able to persuade Bercovitch to come to his tiny Ste. Famille Street flat with the promise of a meal. Afterwards, he showed the reluctant Bercovitch all his canvases, both completed and uncompleted. Bercovitch showed no reaction whatsoever. Borenstein pressed him for an opinion, whereupon Bercovitch suggested he return to school, perhaps to become a doctor. [25]

Plate 19.
From the collection of
Dr. & Mrs. David T. Shizgal

"Boat in Harbour" c. 1936
gouache on paper
35 x 50 cm.

Plate 20.
Private collection

"Der Stumer" (The Mute) 1936
pencil & crayon on cardboard
30 x 23 cm.

By early 1932, Bercovitch was no longer working on a regular basis for Briffa. The Depression had taken hold and even the successful Briffa had to cut back, although he would continue to call on Bercovitch for help with occasional contracts for the next ten years.

Bercovitch was able to find some decorating work, but on a smaller scale, through Philip Hershman, a Montreal housepainter Bercovitch had met at "62 Rachel". (The Communist Party headquarters, often referred to by its address, served as a social centre not only for Party members but for anyone in the immigrant community who cared to come in and use its facilities). [26] The arrangement was a simple one. Hershman would look after all the basic sanding, painting, and wallpapering, and Bercovitch, when needed, would do the decorative work that was fashionable at the time in private homes. It usually took the form of floral decoration in the entrance hall with, sometimes, a mural in the living-room. Bercovitch and Hershman worked together on a number of such contracts through 1932 and the early months of 1933. Bercovitch ate frequently at the home shared by the Hershman and Rudin families on St. Urbain Street and thus saw more of his daughters than he had in earlier years when he was travelling. By this time Bryna and the two girls were living at 3520 Coloniale Avenue, sharing the premises as usual with brother Nachman's "shule". Loneliness appeared to weigh heavily on Bercovitch and, in the summer of 1932, he successfully approached his wife for a reconciliation.

For six months there was a honeymoon, and the house was full of joyful noise. Bryna delighted the girls with impassioned recitations, with Wilde's "Ballad of Reading Gaol" a particular favourite, rendered over the sink with full emphasis and in a heavy Russian accent. To entertain his wife and his daughters, Bercovitch sang nostalgic Russian and Ukrainian songs to his own guitar accompaniment. The family even acquired a second-hand piano, and a Mr. Imminitov was engaged to teach Sylvia music. Better known to Bryna and the girls as Graf Myshkin*, he tore at his hair as students from the "shule" swept shouting in and out of the Bercovitch living-room, piano lessons notwithstanding. The house was full of laughter, and Bercovitch, after a long respite, began once again to paint in earnest.

His first major undertaking was a commission by the well-known Elsie Salomons to produce sets for the three acts of her new ballet, *Benjamin Der Driter* (Benjamin the Third), to be performed by her own company at the Monument National. [27] These would be Bercovitch's first sets since his Habima work ten years earlier. The commission won him much recognition within the Jewish community, and he was introduced to Sarah Caiserman, [28] wife of H.M. Caiserman, founder and secretary of the Canadian Jewish Congress. An accountant by profession and a patron of the arts by avocation, Caiserman was subsidised in his philanthropy by his wife, a successful designer and manufacturer of children's clothes. [29] Caiserman immediately arranged for Bercovitch to give regular private painting lessons to his nine year-old daughter Ghitta.

Bercovitch must have felt optimistic. He moved his family from the "shule" on Coloniale Avenue to a new, more spacious flat at 109 Laurier West. At his request, Bryna stopped teaching. She became home-centred, though she maintained a lively salon of Party and literary friends who spent a great deal of time at her home. Her continued Party connection was a source of extreme irritation to Bercovitch, but, on that point, no compromise was possible.

By the spring of 1933 the honeymoon was over. There was no work available and the household was desperately short of money. Bryna's announcement in April that she was pregnant only worsened the situation. All the old tensions resumed, and Bercovitch flared up again at the Avrutick brothers.

Although Bercovitch and his wife would live together until 1942, through nine more years of quarrels and reconciliations, the nature and pattern of their relationship had by now been irrevocably established. Each had chosen a role and had become trapped in an image. Bercovitch would henceforth present himself to the world as the artist doomed to poverty, shackled by responsibility, and the prey of a nagging and jealous wife. Bryna became the heroine of her own tragedy, combining in her person the eternal victim, the woman-martyr, and the failed Revolution*. For both Bercovitch and Bryna Avrutick life became a drama in which each was the larger-than-life central character. Increasingly, neither would have time for secondary figures like children, except as they might be used as instruments of policy.

It was a difficult period in the Bercovitch home, yet there was an increase in the intensity of Bercovitch's creativity. Whatever their problems, he always painted well while he lived with Bryna.

Soon after the 1932 reconciliation, Bercovitch painted the house on Coloniale Avenue (oil 1932 —

---

* from Dostoevsky's *The Idiot*.

* Bryna left the Communist Party in 1936, some time after the Russian "show-trials", although she remained committed to left-wing ideals.

Top — Cherubs by Bercovitch in the Rialto Theatre, Montreal. Executed in late thirties while Bercovitch was working for Emmanuel Briffa.

Photo: courtesy of Joffre Gendron

Bottom — One of Bercovitch's innumerable sketches as he sat in a St. Lawrence Boulevard café.

(Private collection)

Plate 21.
From the collection of
Jack J. Gordon

"Two Huts on Beach near Percé" 1937
oil on board
43 x 60 cm.

Plate 22.
From the collection of
Mr. & Mrs. Saul Shapiro

"Percé — the Poverty of the Land" c. 1937
gouache on paper
58 x 80 cm.

61

see Plate 10). The brushstroke still has a powerful Russian confidence, but now Bercovitch is painting Canada and not Turkestan. It is a Canadian sky and Canadian snow and a strong Canadian building. Man, expressed in the two dark figures, is enigmatic. Nature is forceful and the trees throw dominating shadows, but the houses have a matching strength.

Man in an urban setting is a theme Bercovitch explored again in "Laurier Avenue" (gouache 1933 — see Plate 23). Possibly Bercovitch's finest urban commentary, it was painted from the balcony of his home. The non-representational people are not only dark accents for the warm sienna and ochre of the buildings, they are also puny figures overshadowed by their environment.

Although Bercovitch was painting as well as he had ever done, he could sell none of his work, neither the new street scenes nor any of the Turkestan works, all still unsold after six years in Canada. The few dollars he received from Caiserman were not enough to pay his rent, and he and his family and his paintings were evicted from his Laurier Avenue home. They moved to poorer accomodation at 4480 de Bullion Street, but rent nonetheless had to be paid. In desperation, Bercovitch phoned the Baron de Hirsch Institute, a constituent of the Federation of Jewish Philanthropies, and Malca Friedman, director of the Welfare Department, sent a young social worker to investigate the family in distress. [30]

Regina Shoolman, the young social worker, was to have a profound effect on the course of Bercovitch's career. She had studied at the Sorbonne at the same time as Louis Muhlstock was painting in Paris, from 1928 to 1931, and she and Muhlstock had become friends. (Much later, after she left Montreal in 1936 to live in New York, she would marry Muhlstock's cousin, Charles Slatkin, and open a successful art gallery.) [31] She had an excellent background in art history, was excited by Bercovitch's work, and was able to persuade Sidney Carter to give Bercovitch a month-long exhibition at the Carter Studio on Drummond Street. She also secured the maximum publicity for her discovery and for the April exhibition. The *Montreal Daily Herald* ran a two-page story on Bercovitch and included a photograph of his "Laurier Avenue"*.

Bercovitch's Montreal career was about to be launched.

---

* The *Daily Herald* article refers to "Laurier Street", as Laurier Avenue was often incorrectly called.

1. Sylvia Bercovitch Ary, in conversation with the author, 1987.

2. Ibid.

3. Ibid.

4. Sylvia remembers how, when the police arrived to break up a mass meeting in 1928, her mother ordered her to hold her ground until the comrades had finished singing the International. She was then five years old.

5. Ruth Pressman, an ardent worker for the Young Communist League in the late twenties and thirties, remembers how all the members were in awe of Bryna, who had participated so actively in the October Revolution. Pressman and Bryna met during the planning stages of *Vestnik* in 1927, soon after Bryna's separation. Montreal interview 19 May 1987.

6. Bryna liked to recite Yiddish poetry at the Kulturcenter's Drama Club (Ruth Pressman interview).

7. Sylvia B. Ary to the author, 1987.

8. Ibid.

9. Louis Muhlstock visited the camp and watched Bercovitch paint the sign (Muhlstock interview, 27 November 1986).

10. Sylvia B. Ary.

11. Information given by Sophie Heyden, 1 June 1987.

12. For details of the life of Emmanuel Briffa (1875-1955), see Dane Lanken, "The Reign of the 'Queens' Draws to a Close," *The Gazette* (Montreal), 13 October 1973. Mr. Lanken also elaborated on Briffa's career in a Montreal interview with the author, 14 July 1987.

13. Joffre Gendron, interviewed in Montreal, 15 July 1987. He is restating a point he made to Dane Lanken in 1973 (see Lanken, "The Reign of the 'Queens'," 13 October 1973). Gendron took over Briffa's contracting company after Briffa died in 1955, and worked until eye problems made retirement obligatory in 1982.

14. Gendron interview, 15 July 1987.

15. There is some disagreement as to which theatre the ticket-booth and the cherubs were in. Gendron, who took the photograph, is sure it was the Rialto; Lanken, theatre historian and *Gazette* film critic from 1967 to 1977, is much less certain. However, both agree with Sylvia Bercovitch Ary that the cherubs were painted by her father.

16. Lanken, "The Reign of the 'Queens'," 13 October 1973.

17. Information in Lanken interview, 14 July 1987.

18. Gendron interview, 15 July 1987.

19. Silverberg's son, David, remembers how, when he was six, in 1942, his mother would leave him at Bercovitch's Prince Arthur Street studio while she shopped. She later explained to him that it was a quid pro quo for the months that Bercovitch had boarded with them in the period 1930 to 1931. In conversation with the author, 12 April 1987.

20. The works exhibited at the Spring Shows of the Art Association of Montreal in 1928 and 1929 (five in 1928 and two in 1929) were all brought from Russia, as were the majority of the works at the 1933 exhibition at the Carter Studio, seven years after Bercovitch arrived in Montreal.

21. Sophie Mayman Heyden interview, 1 June 1987.

22. Interview with Judith Borenstein, Montreal, 25 January 1987. See also William Kuhns and Léo Rosshandler, *Sam Borenstein* (Toronto: McClelland and Stewart, 1978), p. 39.

23. Ibid., p. 39. "It was when Bercovitch showed me his work that I knew I wanted to become a painter."

24. Judith Borenstein, 25 January 1987. After their marriage in 1939, Borenstein told her that he had learned about Van Gogh from Bercovitch. He added that he had discovered Soutine and Vlaminck by himself.

25. Kuhns and Rosshandler, *Sam Borenstein,* p. 40. Bercovitch even attacked Borenstein in the *Kanader Adler.* In the only letter he ever wrote to a newspaper editor, in October 1934, Bercovitch said that "Borenstein cannot draw and cannot paint — everyone knows this and Borenstein himself knows this better than anyone else."

26. Interviews in Montreal with Philip Hershman's son, Hyman, 11 May 1987, and with Philip Hershman's brother-in-law, Morris Rudin, 17 February 1987.

27. Elsie Salomons, interviewed in Montreal, 30 January 1987. The ballet that she wrote and choreographed was about the expulsion of the Jews from a Russian village in the nineteenth century.

28. The introduction was effected by Mrs. Emily "Molly" Mendel. Information given by Mrs. Mendel's daughter, Anita Billick, interviewed in Montreal, 5 April 1987. It appears that Mrs. Mendel was frustrated in her desire to help struggling artists and musicians by her dentist husband, who allowed her no money. All she was able to do was to introduce the artists to possible patrons.

29. Interview with Ghitta Caiserman-Roth, 9 December 1986.

30. Malca Friedman, interviewed in Montreal, 23 June 1987, remembers Regina Shoolman's excitement after her first visit to the Bercovitch home, "I've discovered an artist!".

31. Regina Shoolman Slatkin, in conversation with the author, 11 December 1986.

Plate 23.
From the collection of
Mr. & Mrs. Saul Shapiro

"Laurier Avenue" 1933
gouache on paper
50 x 70 cm.

Eviction Of Artist Brings Recognition

Aleksander Bercovitch "Discovered" as Painter of Merit When He Appeals to Federation of Jewish Philanthropies For Aid — Art Dealer Opens Exhibition For Unrecognized Russian Artist Following Study of Paintings.

Adventurous Career

A 10-year battle with starvation was, up to this week, the reward of Aleksander Bercovitch, painter, for fidelity to his art. His luck came when his landlord called to evict him.

Not given to publicizing his canvasses Bercovitch toiled in obscurity in his little home on Laurier street, unknown to the art public here, his craftsmanship recognized by a few discriminating fellow artists in a similar predicament to himself.

But when the landlord came to evict him, Bercovitch was no longer able, in solitary defence of his little family, to hold out. He appealed to the Federation of Jewish Philanthropies, and in the process was "discovered."

Today a local art dealer opened the first exhibition of his work Montreal has had an opportunity to see.

Not Worth Selling Out Says Landlord

"If I thought all this stuff were worth 50 cents I'd seize it on you," the landlord said when he called to evict him. With a gesture he indicated the paintings that stood all about the room, stacked close to the wall. "As it is I'd rather lose the $30 you owe me than have any further expenses, so if you'll clear out immediately we'll be quits."

The Jewish Philanthropies sent Miss Shoolman, one of their social workers to investigate. She fortunately, had a tutored and discriminating eye. She looked at the "stuff" the landlord disdained, her enthusiasm growing every minutes. Here was an artist! Here was one who could paint with real vigor, who was free of hindering conventions, whose work was not done to the formula of what would sell, who understood drawing, composition, who had originality.

After an hour in the bare little studio, she hurried away to tell her friend, the art dealer, of her discovery. He listened eagerly. Such stories are common enough in books and people talk about finding great artists in garrets struggling superbly without acknowledgment from

(Continued on Page 9)

Russian Painter

Aleksandre Berkovitch, whose newly discovered work is attracting much attention.

Continued from Page 3

the world. . . . He went out to see the collection at once.

The painter, a stalwart man of 39, who strikingly resembles the pictures of Oscar Wilde, received him with modesty and diffidence. Would this man understand his work, or would he be like others to whom he had risked showing his pictures? When his visitor took off his coat and betrayed an animated interest, talked about an exhibition in his galleries, Berkovitch forgot his troubles and became gay.

"This is good," he said, pulling a picture in a raw wood frame from behind others and standing it where his critical guest could see it best. "No, don't bother with that . . . it is a little too realistic . . ."

Born in Cherson Southern Russia

Aleksander Berkovitch was born in Cherson, a town in the south of Russia, which is famous as an art centre. His family were poor, and from the time he was seven or eight years old, he cared for nothing but painting and sketching. While still very young he secured some recognition from the painters to whom he brought his work, and when he was fifteen years old, and earning 200 roubles by making theatrical sets and designing costumes, he went to Palestine to study at the Bezalael School under Professor Schatz, whose aim it was to organize a Jewish school of painting founded on Oriental culture.

That was the beginning of his life as an artist. Manifestly talented, he was given every opportunity. Scholarships were voted to him. When the world war broke out in 1914 he was studying in Munich at the Academy, but he was obliged to return to Russia.

The *Montreal Daily Herald,* Friday 7 April 1933, pp. 3 and 9.

Plate 24.
Private collection

"Laurentian Snow Scene" c. 1938
oil on board
52 x 66 cm.

Plate 25.
From the collection of
Ethel Achtman

"Montreal Street" c. 1939
gouache on paper
17 x 25 cm.

A 1937 art class at the "Y". Bercovitch, standing, has his hand on the easel of Howard Daum. (The gown on the nude behind Bercovitch's head is the addition of the Montreal photographer of the period.)

Photo: courtesy of Howard Daum

CHAPTER FIVE

Critics and Students

The solo exhibition in April 1933 at the Carter Studio was not the first time the Montreal public had seen work by Bercovitch. He had already exhibited at the Spring Show of the Art Association in 1927, 1928, 1929, 1932, and 1933, and four of his canvases had been hung at the Independent Art Association show in October 1932. The Carter exhibition was, however, his first show in a commercial gallery.

The reception by the critics was mixed. Regina Shoolman, not unexpectedly, gave the work great praise. In the *Canadian Jewish Review,* 7 April 1933, she wrote of "Bercovitch's amazing boldness and originality... virility, simplicity, and directness." The critic of *La Presse,* E.R. Bertrand, writing under the pseudonym of "Reynald",[1] was less impressed by what he saw as the "excessive violence of the colours"*, and the "Slav-Oriental" quality of the work (*La Presse,* 4 January 1934). He did not even publish his opinion of the Carter exhibition at the time of its showing, but included his comments as part of his criticism of Bercovitch's second solo exhibition. This took place in December 1933 at the much more prestigious Eaton's Galleries. After eight months of reflection, "Reynald" finally decided that, while Bercovitch was more comfortable in the masculinity of his Turkestan work, he had nevertheless achieved a truth of intention and colour in the Canadian paintings, especially in the Montreal street scenes (see Appendix 5 for the complete review). In a bizarre phrase, intended no doubt as a compliment, "Reynald" praised Bercovitch

for his "semitic" ability to adapt easily to a new environment*.

The art column of the *Montreal Star,* 27 January 1933, unsigned, but almost certainly by Robert Ayre, also compared the Eaton's exhibition favourably to the earlier Carter show. The writer was particularly impressed by the treatment of light in the Canadian work, and by the strength of the Ashkabad portraits (see Appendix 6 for the complete review).

It was Henri Girard who, in *Le Canada,* 5 January 1934, declared himself Bercovitch's most fervent admirer. He was as thrilled by the Montreal work as by that of Turkestan. Both, Girard thought, were created by "an exceptional eye [that]... could see through to the essential truth"** (see Appendix 7 for the complete review).

With very few exceptions, Bercovitch would receive enthusiastic praise from the Montreal critics for the rest of his life. It was his misfortune that Bertrand ("Reynald"), Girard, and Ayre were so far in advance, not only of public taste, but of the opinions of the Royal Academy, the Art Association of Montreal, and the Ecoles des Beaux-Arts.

Ayre[2] and Girard[3] welcomed the influence of the European immigrant painters like Bercovitch, whose humanism they hailed as a counter to the Toronto-based Group of Seven's obsession with Nature. Girard in particular was convinced that the proper study of

---

* "les chocs trop violents de couleurs"

* "Bercovitch montre des rares facultés d'adaptation. C'est par là qu'il doit être sémite"

** "un oeil exceptionnel [qui]... a la faculté de percevoir la vérité authentique d'une chose"

Plate 26.
From the collection of
Harold B. Gordon

"Der Oytzer" (The Treasure) 1939
gouache & pastel on paper
44 x 85 cm.

Plate 27.
Private collection

"Two Gangsters" 1940
oil on board
68 x 54 cm.

the artist was Man. [4] Although he opposed the idea of Art for Art's sake, he could accept Expressionist distortion and even a degree of Abstraction provided that the painter did not concern himself with Nature. Girard defended the modernism of both Bercovitch and Brandtner because each was "a sincere interpreter of the concerns of our day"*. [5] In Bercovitch and the other Europeans, Girard saw "the French soul", [6] bringing to Québec the best of European culture to serve as a bulwark against those American and British influences which threatened to destroy the "European" nature of French Canada. [7] Girard loved the strength of Bercovitch's painting, and contrasted it with the saccharin and sentimental prettiness he found in Academy-approved work. [8]

E.R. Bertrand ("Reynald") was the most cautious of the critics. He could deplore "excessive urbanization", while at the same time claiming that "nothing touches us more than the city"**. [9] He was more afraid of experiment than was Girard, and he even spoke of the "nightmares" of Fritz Brandtner, [10] but, by 1937, he felt able to commit himself and, in a remarkable essay of apology for his previous doubts, "Réintroduction au modernisme," *La Presse,* 9 October 1937, he welcomed Modern Art to Québec.

Robert Ayre, who wrote for all the English-language papers and journals of the period, including the *Montrealer,* the *Standard, Saturday Night,* and the *Star,* held an unchanging position, critical both of the Royal Canadian Academy and of the tired repetitions of the Group of Seven. He was always generous in his praise of Bercovitch and the other newcomers.

In spite of the excellent reviews and the unflagging efforts of his self-appointed publicist, Regina Shoolman, Bercovitch sold very little work. Shoolman, who never lost faith, continued her campaign. She introduced the painter to notables in the Jewish community, like the poet and lawyer A.M. Klein, whose portrait he painted, "Mr. and Mrs. A.M. Klein" (oil 1934 — see Plate 12). She also made Bercovitch welcome at the salon she held at her Côte Ste. Catherine Road apartment where her other guests included the writer-poet Sol Pomerance, the radio-dramatist Robert Choquette, and the novelist Alain Grandbois. Bercovitch was considerably handicapped by his shyness and always tried to avoid speaking to the others, much preferring to meet Pomerance later on St. Lawrence where, as Pomerance remembers, they "ingested" smoked-meat sandwiches together at Rogatko's. [11]

It was at this time that Bercovitch met Blanche and Honoré Parent who would become his only real Canadian patrons. Madame Parent was a prominent member of the influential women's group, La Société d'Etudes et Conférences, and had heard the critic Henri Girard speak glowingly of Bercovitch at one of their meetings. [12] She and her lawyer husband [13] invited Bercovitch and his wife to dinner and asked to see his work. The Parents were impressed and, after commissioning a portrait of Honoré Parent, they bought two of the works from Turkestan (see Plates 5 and 6). (The bank phoned the next day to ask if the Parents had indeed issued a cheque for $100.00 to a "heavy Russian of unkempt appearance.") Bercovitch was elated. The Parents treated him with great respect, and both he and they regarded the gifts and Christmas hampers they pressed upon him for the next ten years as the rightful homage that friends pay to an admired artist. It was all so different from the left-over food and unwanted old clothes that arrived occasionally from the neighbours and community dignitaries as heavy-handed and much-trumpeted charity. There were few sales other than to the Parents, [14] but Bercovitch felt a renewed confidence that manifested itself in the work of the period. In the compelling "Path in Park" (oil c. 1934 — see Plate 14) there is the same powerful divided brushstroke as in the Ashkabad paintings, but the study in green is strongly and undeniably Canadian.

Bercovitch had cause for cautious optimism until, in the spring of 1934, his health failed. Already overweight and a victim of hayfever, [15] he suffered a severe bout of rheumatic fever. His home was full of children and tension, and he felt a desperate need of change. The birth of a son, Joshua Sacvan*, on October 4, 1933, had pleased him — he had wanted a son — but he was impatient with his family's needs and the house was more crowded than ever. The excursions to Miss Shoolman's were not enough, especially since the resentful and possibly jealous Bryna had taken to sending Sylvia to cut short the revelry and to bring her father home. Sylvia, like the Greek messenger, often had to bear the brunt of her father's wrath at being so disturbed.

In the summer of 1934, with the proceeds of the Parent sales, Bercovitch went alone on the first of his many visits to the Gaspé Peninsula. [16] It was love at first sight and his "Point-au-Père" (oil c. 1934 — see Plate 15) was only one of the innumerable studies he would make of the Percé area over the years.

There was excellent news waiting for Bercovitch when he finally got back to Montreal, much re-

---

* "sincère interprète de l'inquiétude de notre époque"
** "il faut déplorer l'urbanisation excessive [mais]... rien n'est plus près de nous que la cité"

---

* the name is a compression of "Sacco" and "Vanzetti"

freshed. It was sufficient even to lift the hopes of his family, for whom he had made no financial provision during his absence. Regina Shoolman had been made Executive Director of the YWHA and wanted Bercovitch to teach the art classes she was instituting in the coming winter session. (Initially two evenings a week, they were later expanded to include a Sunday class.) [17]

Bercovitch would give classes at the Y from 1934 to 1946, and would teach a whole generation of Montreal Jewish artists. Some would have studied with Anne Savage at the local Baron Byng High School — and it is inevitable that they would make comparisons — but for many Bercovitch would be their first and only art teacher.

Almost without exception, his students remember him fondly. In that first 1934-35 class was Trudy Sack, who later went on to live and paint in Greenwich Village. Her memory of the class in the Y attic is of ten young men and women in the care of "a sweet, gentle man".

> His enthusiasm was unbelievable; everyone had ability, he thought. No one could match his involvement. He never bought a cigarette and would constantly ask for one. He would light up and would sit down to help with our drawings or paintings. He would put the cigarette on the bench (never in an ashtray) or flick the ashes all over his clothes. He became so engrossed in his efforts that the cigarette would burn to ashes. We all loved him and tried in our limited way to help him to sell his work... He seemed so vulnerable because of his naiveté and the excitement and enthusiasm he projected when we applied colours that were harmonious... In my recollections [of eight years of classes with him] I cannot remember that he 'put down' anyone's work. [18]

It appears that Bercovitch was as gentle to his students as he was acerbic to his fellow-artists. [19]

In the same class as Trudy Sack was Moe Reinblatt, who continued at the Y with Bercovitch until 1941, often acting as his "massier"*. Reinblatt left Montreal in 1941 to serve as an official war artist in Europe, but resumed a close relationship with Bercovitch after his demobilisation in 1945. Moe Reinblatt had been Anne Savage's first male art student at Baron Byng

High School, but, like Rita Briansky, [20] who also studied with both Savage and Bercovitch, Reinblatt felt that he owed far more to Bercovitch. From Bercovitch he learned not only his love of portraits, [21] but, in his own words, "how to look, how to see, how to draw, how to paint." [22] Reinblatt's mother had died when he was very young, and he had been brought up by an older sister and a father who could spare little time away from his embroidery factory. [23] In Bercovitch he found the kind, attentive adult he had longed for. In his 1951 tribute to his mentor, Reinblatt wrote:

> He was not a formalist, either in theory or technique. He understood abstract art but felt, as does de Segonzac, that it is the structure upon which all great painting is built and not an end in itself. Bercovitch was too moved by the visual aspect of the world to turn inward solely for his inspiration. He was too anxious to communicate simply with others. This impulse to share made him a good teacher from whom one learned to have an abiding love of art... He was one of that brave company of men who live enough in their art to sacrifice all the comforts of everyday life so that they may discover the world for others to see and take pleasure in. It is always a warming and heartening revelation of the courage and the will to expression of the human spirit. It brings us solace and inspiration. [24]

Eudice Garmaise, later a painter and teacher, who took Bercovitch's Y classes from 1935 to 1939 and who shared a studio for twenty years with Reinblatt, remembers Bercovitch as

> an immensely understanding and encouraging teacher — we all loved him. It was he, with Fritz Brandtner, who brought Expressionism to Québec. [25]

Morton Pesner, a prominent Montreal businessman who remembers his private lessons from Bercovitch in 1941 and 1942 after a year of art classes at the Y, echoes the praise:

> I adored him. He was a hands-on teacher. He held the hand and brush to show you what to do. He was very giving in time and talent, a very warm, gentle, kind, patient man... a far greater teacher than Anne Savage. [26]

---

* a kind of class manager, responsible for setting up, posing the model, etc.

Plate 28.
Private collection

"Gaspé: Cliff and Sea" c. 1940
watercolour on paper
44 x 58 cm.

Plate 29.
From the collection of
Mr. & Mrs. Saul Shapiro

"Untitled Nude" 1942
pastel on paper
110 x 58 cm.

Rosalie Goodman Namer, who studied at the Y in 1941-1942 and privately with Bercovitch from 1942 to 1944, says that:

> Bercovitch was the total artist. There was nothing else. He was a great teacher. He was an Expressionist, but he didn't try to change me, to make me like him. What I learned from him was that my commitment was right. [27]

Bercovitch gave Namer the same advice he had earlier given Moe Reinblatt, "an artist should not marry." [28] He elaborated on the theme: "You will not continue to paint if you get married. You'll have children. It might work only if you marry another artist." Namer reflects that Bercovitch may have been right: "I did nothing for several years, and, when I came back, it was to ceramics, not to painting." [29]

Rita Briansky, who would later receive critical acclaim for her many solo exhibitions in Montreal, Toronto, Ottawa, and Winnipeg, recalls her first nervous day in Bercovitch's Y class in 1941. She had drawn from infancy, had stolen school chalk to draw on the sidewalks, but had never before seen original art or met an artist. [30] Bercovitch, portly, with bulging eyes, a black silk ascot, and black, soupstained clothes, was exactly what she had dreamed of, "the ultimate bohemian".

> What he gave me [in the classes from 1941 to 1944] was infinitely more valuable than what I found later with any other teacher I had, either here in Montreal or at the Art Students' League in New York. He was inarticulate without a brush in his hand. His English was basic — 'not like that, like this' — 'skin is like this, hair is like that' — always with accompanying gestures, but his lessons have always remained with me. He was very kind. [31]

Jack J. Gordon, a Montreal entrepreneur but a painter by avocation, was Bercovitch's student at the Y from 1938 to 1940 and his friend and admirer ever after. He has the same memory as Briansky of Bercovitch's instructions:

> They were elementary phrases, but they never left you. Bercovitch would say, pointing, 'I know it is a cheek because it is below the eye. But where is the bone? Where is the flesh?' [32]

Ghitta Caiserman, now an artist of considerable national standing, remembers, still with some asperity, that Bercovitch did not hesitate to embellish her paintings. To one of her portraits, that of Jerome Myers in 1938, Bercovitch added a line of ballet-dancers in the background. [33] It was not until much later that she realised how much she owed to her teacher. She also remembers envying Moe Reinblatt the intimacy he seemed to enjoy with Bercovitch, but now thinks that "perhaps it took a man to tolerate Bercovitch's lack of care in his personal appearance." [34]

The celebrated sculptor Esther Wertheimer, a painting student at the Y from 1941 to 1946, has a precise recollection of Bercovitch's encouragement:

> He was the first person to start me working seriously. He showed me how to work with a limited palette. A master draughtsman, he could capture everything in a line. He was inarticulate, but he showed me what I needed to know with just a gesture... I was very grateful. Bercovitch took me under his wing... I could always bring my work to show him... He had a perfect eye: he was a master of seeing and recording. [35]

Bercovitch's manifest love of the act of creation was an inspiration to his students. Howard Daum, a Y student in 1936 and 1937, was motivated by Bercovitch to begin a fifty year career as an artist. As Daum writes from New York:

> To me, the process was important, this act of something becoming. I've never seen anyone show this better than Bercovitch. To this day, the adventure of the process of creating always remains with me. [36]

Not all of Bercovitch's students went on to gain great reputations after they left his classes. Some, like Harry Allister or Ida Cramer Allister, would continue to paint only for recreation, but all would share a memory of a man who was "naive, guileless, non-worldly, warm, and innocent, yet capable of passion." [37]

What his students saw and loved in Bercovitch was his uncompromising belief in the value of his work. On one occasion there was some discussion as to whether, in his portrait of Sam Bronfman, Bercovitch had completely captured the great man's likeness. "What does it matter if it is or if it is not Bronfman?" growled the artist. "What matters is that it is a Bercovitch." [38]

Bercovitch could be wilful and unpredictable,

but the love he engendered in his students could withstand the most rigorous of tests.

Jack J. Gordon remembers the fiasco of the painting trip to Maine. Gordon had long dreamed of painting with his former teacher along the New England coast, and, to that end, invited Bercovitch to come with him on an all-expense-paid holiday. It was to take place in the early summer of 1947, before Bercovitch left his winter quarters in Montreal to go to Camille and his beloved Percé.

After the long drive to Ogunquit, in a borrowed car piled high with empty canvases, Bercovitch announced that "the stones of Maine pale before the majesty of the Gaspé," and refused to paint. He demanded instead that they tour the small art galleries of the resort area. At each stop Bercovitch maintained a loud, continuous, and unflattering commentary on all the works on show. The word "banal", his favourite when speaking of other artists, figured large. To the heightened indignation of the gallery-owners, and to the extreme embarrassment of his student, Bercovitch also insisted on touching the exhibits whenever he wanted to check a texture or to demonstrate a flaw in technique. It was a saddened though no less devoted young man who drove the unrepentant Bercovitch back to Montreal, with every canvas as blank as when they had left.[39]

The most complete assessment of Bercovitch the teacher is perhaps that of Pearl Garfinkle Leibovitch, in a tribute published four years after Bercovitch's death. An art student at the Y in 1936, she later became a social worker and the wife of the painter Norman Leibovitch. She wrote very specifically of her debt to her old teacher:

> Bercovitch, for most of us, seemed one of the few links with the broader world of pictures and ideas. We responded intuitively to the strength and vigour of his work. Critical of the world around us, we were easily sympathetic to this man in middle age who seemed never to have accepted or learned to adjust to authority himself.

> Romantic, emotional, rather confused in his own life, he maintained his position doggedly; the position of the creative individual who bases his claim to integrity on the fulfilment of his creative task, for

better or worse; to be himself and to survive as an artist. Indeed, it was this insistence alone that could have laid an effective claim on our loyalty to him as a teacher. Possibly, his shabbiness and obvious lack of material success helped make his influence all the more poignant.

> He tended to be sharp and uncompromising in his criticisms of art and behaviour, and there were angry and quixotic strains in his nature that deviated his ideas, so we learned a sort of protective hesitation in accepting his opinions wholesale; but what we gained from him as a teacher was real and clear. He saw the artist as dignified by his art and viewed his own task as a painter as a compelling endeavour. This he felt with passion and intensity, and he marked us all as a result. Inarticulate as he sometimes seemed, he conveyed to us the most important thing a teacher can give, a sense of the worth and a belief in the value of art. In retrospect, this remains; this and the paintings. His paintings are evocative in colour and in form. Look at a painting of Percé Rock, majestic and dramatic, with a silver-white woman's head dreaming in the foreground, or the head of a boy, or a certain quality of blue in one painting, and a tremendous burst of flowers in another; but go back and look again and the rock seems a simple mass painted in roughly, the boy's head — how is that still, timeless sense conveyed? — the blue is just blue, and the flowers, — what makes them sing out so across the room?

> And as it is with the paintings, so it is with the man. Perhaps because he marked us when impressions are vivid and the imagination plastic. Close up, the contradictions were apparent, the marks of defeat and struggle, of defensiveness and loneliness; but looming there in the distance of the mind, as I remember the paintings, I remember the man, the artist, and the teacher — as I remember the rock and the flowers.[40]

Plate 30.
From the collection of
Jack J. Gordon

"Petrushka" 1946
oil on gold paint on canvas
200 x 478 cm.

1. For the real name of "Reynald", I am indebted to Esther Trépanier, Professor of Art History at l'Université du Québec à Montréal, interviewed in Montreal, 29 November 1986. See also Yvan Lamonde and Esther Trépanier, *L'avènement de la modernité culturelle au Québec* (Montréal: Institut Québécois de Recherche sur la Culture, 1986), p. 107.

2. See, inter alia, Ayre, " 'Art of Our Day' Attracting Attention by Its Vigour in Design," *Montreal Standard*, 27 May 1939, and Ayre, " 'Fundamental' and Other Views on Canvas: Second Thoughts on Canadian Group Show," *Montreal Standard*, 13 January 1940.

3. Lamonde and Trépanier, *L'avènement de la modernité culturelle*, p. 82.

4. Girard asserted that "Man should regain pride of place in Canadian painting" ("que l'homme reprenne dans la peinture canadienne la place prépondérante"), *Le Canada*, 1 March 1933, and that the purpose of art was to communicate "une image profonde et véritable de l'homme," *Le Canada*, 25 January 1939.

5. Girard, "Fritz Brandtner à la Galerie Morgan," *Le Canada*, 26 February 1936.

6. Girard, "Alexandre Bercovitch à la Galerie Eaton," *Le Canada*, 5 January 1934.

7. Girard, "L'école de Paris," *Le Canada*, 22 October 1936.

8. Lamonde and Trépanier, *L'avènement de la modernité culturelle*, p. 85.

9. "Reynald", "Les inspirations du milieu social," *La Presse*, 20 February 1935.

10. "Reynald", "Les cauchemars de Fritz Brandtner," *La Presse*, 22 February 1936.

11. Sol Pomerance, interviewed in Montreal, 4 June 1987.

12. Blanche Parent, interviewed in Montreal, 11 December 1986.

13. In 1928, Honoré Parent had represented the City of Montreal before the British Privy Council in what was only the first of many important pleadings. In 1960 Parent became the chief counsel for the City of Montreal.

14. A rare exception was Saul Shapiro, interviewed in Montreal, 20 January 1987, who bought "Laurier Avenue" after the 1933 Eaton's exhibition not because of its artistic merit or the favourable reviews, but because his fiancée had lived at 124 Laurier West. Later, Shapiro bought more Bercovitch work and, in 1949, commissioned two illustrations for a privately-bound book of poetry as well as a portrait of his two sons (see Plates 32, 33, and 35).

15. The hayfever was not a lifelong allergy. In a letter to Bercovitch, 17 November 1945, Sigmund Lev, formerly the director of the Theatre League, congratulates Bercovitch for reporting that he no longer had the problem. Author's files.

16. Charles Hill, in *Canadian Painting in the Thirties*, p. 130, is wrong in suggesting that Bercovitch first visited the Gaspé in 1935.

17. *History of the Montreal YM-YWHA*, ed. Sherry Stein, p. 9, and supplementary information from Regina Shoolman Slatkin, interviewed 11 December 1986.

18. Letter to the author from Trudy Sack, 31 May 1987.

19. His cruelty to Sam Borenstein, who so admired him, is well documented (see Chapter 4, footnote 25), and there is much evidence of the same quality in his everyday humour, even when in jest with a friend. Allan Harrison, whom he first met in the Gaspé in 1938, tells an interesting story. Bercovitch had asked to look at one of his paintings and Harrison had declined with a modest 'No, I'd rather not, it's lousy.' Finally Harrison gave in and showed the picture. With his hand on his stomach instead of his heart, Bercovitch said, 'On my word of honour that's a lousy picture.' Allan Harrison, in conversation with the author, Montreal, 1 December 1986.

20. Rita Briansky, interviewed in Montreal, 7 December 1986.

21. Information from Eudice Garmaise, interviewed in Montreal, 10 December 1986. Garmaise, who had herself studied at the Y with Bercovitch from 1935 to 1939, shared a studio with Reinblatt from 1959 to 1979. The information was confirmed by Lilian Reinblatt, interviewed in Montreal, 17 February 1987. Lilian, like her husband, had also studied with Anne Savage at Baron Byng High School.

22. This was often repeated by Reinblatt to Garmaise in their shared studio (Garmaise interview, 10 December 1986).

23. Garmaise interview.

24. Moe Reinblatt, "Aleksandre Bercovitch 1893-1951," *Canadian Art*, 8 (Spring 1951), pp. 110-111. (Reinblatt made an error with the date of birth.)

25. Garmaise interview, 10 December 1986.

26. Morton Pesner, interviewed in Montreal, 7 April 1987, had studied with Anne Savage in 1938.

27. Rosalie Goodman Namer, interviewed in Montreal, 20 April 1987, switched from painting to ceramics in 1948. She was one of the first students of the new Ceramics Department of Montreal's Ecole du Meuble. The department was set up by Pierre Normandeau of the Sèvres factory, and Namer was the first ceramicist in Canada to try the now widely used technique of reduction firing.

28. Lilian Reinblatt interview, 17 February 1987. Apparently Moe took his teacher's advice to heart. Although he and Lilian met in 1936, they did not marry until 1943. Moe then told Lilian of Bercovitch's earlier advice.

29. Namer interview, 20 April 1987.

30. Rita Briansky interview, 7 December 1986. Briansky had led a sheltered childhood, living with her parents in small towns in northern Ontario after coming from Poland to Canada in 1924. She arrived in Montreal in 1941. It was Ida Maze (a.k.a. Massey), a well-known "macher" (one who makes things happen) in the Yiddish-speaking community, who persuaded Briansky's parents to allow her to study with Bercovitch. Mrs. Maze was a rival to Bryna Bercovitch in her ability to gather creative people around her, although Mrs. Maze's "salon", unlike that of Bryna, was apolitical. A minor poet herself, Ida Maze did what she could for artists in need, sometimes with more compassion than discrimination. Ethel Achtman, interviewed 18 April 1987, was only one of many who overheard Mrs. Maze's revealing comment on a would-be Jewish writer, "Er hot nisht kein brekl talant. Men muz im helfn aroisgeben a bukh" (He is without a crumb of talent. We must help him to publish a book). (It is only fair to note that Rita Briansky, for one, believes that the remark was made in jest.) Apparently, Mrs. Maze was not the only community leader to let her enthusiasm run away with her. The poet J.I. Segal said of H.M. Caiserman, "when Caiserman sees a native Montreal or Toronto Jew write a few simple verses, he is enthralled... Why Caiserman is not more circumspect in his appraisal of the artistic world is still incomprehensible to me." See Bernard Figler and David Rome,

Hannaniah Meir Caiserman: a Biography (Montreal: Northern Printing, 1962), p. 195.

31. Briansky interview.

32. Jack J. Gordon, interviewed in Montreal, 27 November 1986, and 25 May 1987.

33. During an interview in Montreal, 25 January 1987, Jerome and Zelda Myers showed the author the 1938 Caiserman portrait of Jerome to which Bercovitch had added the line of dancers.

34. Ghitta Caiserman-Roth, interviewed in Montreal, 9 December 1986.

35. Esther Wertheimer, interviewed in Montreal, 28 May 1987, switched from painting to sculpture when she went to Italy to study in 1967.

36. Letter from Howard Daum to the author, 15 May 1987.

37. Both interviewed in Montreal, 25 January 1987. Harry Allister studied at the Y from 1941 to 1942, and Ida (Cramer) from 1934 to 1936.

38. Jack J. Gordon interview, 27 November 1986. Gordon was not present when Bercovitch made the comment. Bercovitch told him about the incident later, in early 1947. The story is therefore apocryphal.

39. Jack J. Gordon interview, 25 May 1987.

40. Pearl Leibovitch, "Aleksandre Bercovitch, A Recollection of The Man, The Artist, The Teacher," *Canadian Jewish Review,* 16 September 1955, pp. 12, 134. I am grateful to Pearl Garfinkle Leibovitch for drawing my attention to her article when we spoke together in Montreal on 2 February 1987, just weeks before her death.

Plate 31.
From the collection of
Harold B. Gordon

"Moishele Geller, Cantor" 1946
oil on board
95 x 58 cm.

82

CHAPTER SIX

Montreal: 1935-1936

As the year 1935 began, Bercovitch was enjoying the first of many winter seasons teaching at the Y and was busy preparing his students for their first exhibition in May.[1] In a corner of the St. Dominique Street flat he was painting those "subtlely composed and richly coloured portraits in the tradition of Cézanne" that Paul Duval so admired.[2] Two such portraits are those of "Assya" (oil c. 1935 — see Plate 18) and "Sue Boroff" (oil c. 1935 — see Plate 17).[3] Both portraits are built with heavy single strokes, a technique much admired by Bercovitch's students. (Moe Reinblatt's early portraits are very similar in this respect to those of his teacher.) The brushstrokes are enlarged almost to the point of becoming planes of colour, while the whole concept is realized, as Ernst Neumann observed, with "a technique of draughtsmanship capable of depicting the subtleties of character."[4]

Not all of Bercovitch's portraits were affectionate. In December 1934, Bryna's brother Nachman arranged for Bercovitch to paint the portrait of Nachman's doctor, Harold Segall. Bercovitch could hardly turn away the much-needed business and he accepted the commission in spite of his aversion to his Avrutick in-laws. After only a very few sittings, Bercovitch called his subject to come and collect the finished article. Segall and his wife hurried over only to find a horrid caricature in discordant greens. Segall, who refused the painting, theorizes that "Bercovitch put all his hatred of the Avruticks into the work. They had been kind to him for far too long and the burden of an unpaid debt is intolerable."[5]

Bercovitch still found it difficult to sell his work, and Emmanuel Briffa, the cinema decorator, was calling on his services only rarely. The income from the few private lessons and the Y classes was insufficient to maintain the artist and his family. He was a Jewish painter in a French Catholic province, controlled economically by an English Protestant minority, and it is impossible to avoid considering the phenomenon of anti-semitism and the degree to which it might have contributed to Bercovitch's financial distress.

Ethnic boundaries in Quebec in 1935 were clearly defined and almost never crossed. The English kept very much to themselves, and the resort hotels they patronised in the Laurentians often displayed anti-Jewish slogans.[6] There is no record of an "English" Montrealer buying any work from Bercovitch at this time, though it should be pointed out, in fairness, that the English bought little art from anyone — except their own portraits from Alphonse Jongers.

The relationship of the Jews to the French-speaking Catholic majority was much more complex.

The Church in Québec had been sympathetic to Italian Fascism since the Mussolini-Vatican Concordat of 1929, and any suspicions it had harboured about the German variety had been largely allayed when Pope Pius XI and Hitler came to their understanding in 1933. In that same year in Québec, the Fascist leader Adrien Arcand was receiving the support not only of the ultra-nationalist St. Jean Baptiste Society but also of the organizer of the provincial Conservative Party ($27,000.00 in subsidies between 1930 and 1933, specifically for Arcand's three anti-Jewish newspapers).[7] Also in 1933, the abbé Lionel Groulx, a virulent anti-semite, helped to launch two xenophobic movements, the Action Nationale and its Université de Montréal-centred junior auxiliary, Les Jeune-Canada. Both were dedicated to the boycott of Jewish businesses, with the slogan "Achat Chez Nous" (Buy From Your Own), and to the refusal of refuge to German Jews. Father Groulx had the support of such influential newspapers as *Le Devoir, L'Action Catholique,* and *Le Droit,*[8] and his message was clear; "one finds the Jew at the bottom of every shady deal, every kind of pornographic business."*[9]

The call to hatred was not, of course, universally received. Bercovitch himself had already been welcomed into the Parent circle and later, after 1941, would find great and lasting friendships among both clergy and Catholic laity in Québec City and Joliette.

Esther Trépanier, a professor of Art History at the Université du Québec, points out that, although the world of her childhood seems to have been Catholic and conservative at best, and racist if not fascist at worst, there were so many exceptions that the single governing image is misleading. Québec society was more complex than that. She contrasts her own memory with that of a Montreal Jewish friend of the same age who told her, "But, when I was young, *everybody* was Left!"[10] Such was the isolation, one from another, of Québec's cultural solitudes.

It is not possible to know the extent to which Bercovitch and the other Québec artists were penalised because of this ghettoization. Charles Maillard, Director of the Ecole des Beaux-Arts in Montreal, was known to associate Jews with Bolshevism and modern art,[11] and Ernst Neumann may have been right when he told his model, Madeleine Boyer, in 1937, that Maillard had refused him a teaching post because he was Jewish.[12] Bercovitch himself was passed over in favour of Goodridge Roberts when both applied for the same teaching job at the Art Association of Montreal in 1939. It is true that Bercovitch had a slight stammer, but Goodridge Roberts was absolutely inarticulate and rarely even tried to speak.[13]

Such anger as Bercovitch felt at his failure to sell was directed more against his own immigrant community than against the English or the French. Judith Borenstein comments that "he was justifiably bitter. All the Jewish community gave him were a few dollars as a Y teacher,"[14] and Bryna's friend, Ruth Pressman, adds that "the few [in the community] who had money quibbled about price."[15]

Bercovitch's most pressing concern as the summer of 1935 approached was not how to overcome the legacy of centuries of anti-semitism, but how to finance a second summer visit to the Gaspé Peninsula. After much reflection he made a plan, and it was bold. Using his daughter Sylvia as his secretary (he never learned to write English well, and his French was non-existent), he addressed himself to Vincent Massey, the Governor-General of Canada. The proposition was a simple one: Massey would provide $100.00 for Bercovitch's summer expenses, and Bercovitch would allow Massey to choose the best of the Gaspé work. Bercovitch provided an impressive curriculum vitae, and Massey was taken with the artist's daring. The upshot was that Bercovitch went to the village of Percé with the Governor-General's $100.00, neglecting once again to leave any money with his wife and children in Montreal. Massey later asked H.O. McCurry, Assistant Director of the National Gallery, to select a Bercovitch landscape for him. Since McCurry admired Bercovitch's earlier work, but did not like the Gaspé paintings, there was a prolonged correspondence between Massey, McCurry, and Bercovitch from December 1935 to May 1936. During this period, Massey *bought* a Bercovitch landscape at the Sidney Carter Gallery in Montreal. It is not clear if McCurry ever made a final selection or if Massey ever received a painting for his $100.00.[16]

After a productive summer, Bercovitch came back to Montreal with enough canvases for a third solo exhibition. It was held at the Eaton's Galleries in October and November and the critics were divided. Girard, in *Le Canada,* was horrified that Bercovitch had devoted himself so completely to landscapes. He feared that Bercovitch had submitted to the pressure of the Group of Seven, and called on him to forget his "Gaspé nightmares". (His fury was, fortunately, short-lived: Girard could not be angry with Bercovitch for long.)[17] "Reynald" of *La Presse,* usually reluctant to commit himself, gave the exhibition unreserved praise and delighted in quoting and in disagreeing with Girard. "Reynald" declared that Bercovitch had presented the "authentic face"* of the Gaspé in a series of paintings that was outstanding for its vigour, its honesty, its varied palette, and its intensity of feeling.[18]

The following year, 1936, was one of Bercovitch's fullest (for a complete list of his exhibitions after 1926 see back of book). In January, he was invited to contribute to the Canadian Group of Painters' travel-

---

* "il arrive de trouver le Juif au fond de toutes les affaires louches, de toutes les entreprises de pornographie"

* "visage authentique, tonifiant, profond"

ling exhibition, beginning at the Art Gallery of Toronto, and, in March, as a "distinguished guest", he exhibited two canvases with the Ontario Society of Artists at the same gallery. Charles Hill said of one of the works, "The Artist's Family" (oil 1934 — see Plate 13), that "the roughly applied paint has an Expressionist intensity, accentuated by the confinement and monumentality of the figures."[19] In April, Bercovitch sent works to the "Canadian and European Art" Exhibition at the Watson Gallery, and in May, to the "Survey of Canadian Art" at W. Scott & Sons. His work was accepted both at the Spring Show of the Art Association of Montreal and at the Royal Academy Fall Exhibition in Toronto. With six exhibitions in one year, and with his Y students' second show in December, Bercovitch in 1936 was as active as a Montreal painter could be.

He was painting at a furious pace, and had begun to spend his weekends at Val Morin as the guest of Fanny Lazar and her friend, the painter Lionel Fielding Downes. Fanny Lazar, a Montrealer who rented a summer cottage in the late thirties and early forties for herself and her grandchildren, fed Bercovitch in return for painting lessons.[20] He and "Bill" Downes slept in a nearby shack on the property. "Val Morin — Lake and Trees" (oil c. 1936 — see Plate 16) is typical of his summer work in the Laurentians. It is an Impressionist treatment of the play of light on water. In spite of the governing mood of the painting, one of serenity, there is an exciting underlying tension that derives from the counterpoint of vertical and horizontal brushstrokes, shorter than was usual in Bercovitch's work, and more animated because of the compression.

In addition to his painting, Bercovitch had long been involved with costume and set design for a number of Jewish theatre groups. Drama, amateur or otherwise, was very popular in the community, and groups would put on not only the work of such established names as Sholem Aleichem, but also plays written by their own members. Particularly popular were the didactic melodramas offered by the Communist Party. The message never changed — the rich exploit the poor — but the stories came out of the audience's own experience. One of the greatest of the Party's theatrical successes was its 1935 production of *Die Chappers* by Chaver Paver*. Set in Russia, it was about the period when rich Jews would bribe the Tsarist authorities to avoid conscription. Since the Jewish quota had to be filled, a press-gang, "die chappers" (the catchers), would fall upon the poor of

the neighbourhood. The victims had to serve for twenty-five years in the Tsar's army, after which they were fit only to sing in the streets for their bread.[21]

Bercovitch's set and costume designs were always imaginative and often Expressionist, but he was designing for groups that met in basements, and there was never a budget large enough for anything but the most basic realization of his original intention. He was a long way from the splendour of the Odessa Opera House or the Habima Theatre in Moscow.

There is little visual record of his work in the Montreal Jewish theatre, but his 1936 costume designs for *Die Oreme Meluche* (The Kingdom of the Poor)[22] still survive, including his sketch of "Der Stumer" (The Mute) (pencil & crayon 1936 — see Plate 20), as much a study of character as it is of costume.

Fortunately, his magnificent city backdrop for the 1938 *Winterset* was photographed by one of the cast,[23] and he was so pleased with his set for *Der Oytzer* (The Treasure) in 1939[24] that he made a pastel and gouache representation of it for himself (see Plate 26) which he never offered for sale. It came on the market only after his death.

It was in the middle thirties that Bercovitch began to paint those harbour scenes that Louis Muhlstock saw as "brilliant — immediate and spontaneous".[25] Sometimes, as in the extremely complex "Boat in Harbour" (gouache c. 1936 — see Plate 19), he was concerned with solving the technical problems of naturalistic composition; and sometimes he made a social statement, as with the painterly "Harbour Scene" (gouache and pastel c. 1938 — see Plate 11) in which the colours are those of industry and the sky is an extension of the smoke. Even when he was surrounded by the natural beauty of the Gaspé Peninsula, Bercovitch, although a political skeptic, would occasionally be moved to make a comment on the human condition. "Percé — the Poverty of the Land" (gouache c. 1937 — see Plate 22) is such a study, although the mood, expressed through the transparency and melancholy of the colours, is lyrical, and the head is a reminder of the ikons of Bercovitch's youth.

Unless he was working on a painting at home, Bercovitch rarely spent the day with his family. As his daughter Sylvia remembers:

> He would get up in the morning, not very early and usually in a gloomy and taciturn mood. After breakfast he would go out. His mood lightened as he put on his flowing black silk tie, his heavy, dark coat, and his black velour hat. As he went towards the

---

* an alliterative pen-name, punning on the word "chaver" (comrade)

A.Bercovitch

Plate 32.
From the collection of
Mr. & Mrs. Saul Shapiro

"Eve" 1948
book illustration
20 x 15 cm.

Plate 33.
From the collection of
Mr. & Mrs. Saul Shapiro

"Negress" 1948
book illustration
20 x 15 cm.

door, moving quickly and lightly for all his heaviness, he would begin to hum a little tune. [26]

When he left the house, his huge pockets were stuffed with pads, pencils, erasers, penknives, and crayons. Bercovitch believed that an artist should draw constantly. On a fine day, he went to sketch at the waterfront or on Mount Royal. If the weather was inclement, he would meet his friends at Mayman's store or at one of the St. Lawrence Boulevard restaurants. Essentially a shy man, he preferred public places to people's homes, and he dearly loved to watch and draw the passing show. Café life was colourful and noisy and exciting, and peopled with characters like Moishe Leib Hershunov. It was Moishe Leib who, to Bercovitch's delight, put his own obituary in the newspaper and then hid opposite the funeral home to see who would come to mourn him. [27]

Bercovitch came home even less frequently after he rented a "studio" in September 1936. A pitifully small room behind a Bible store at 76 Prince Arthur Street East, it nevertheless provided the painter with a refuge from the responsibilities that he seemed unable to accept. In 1938 he took over the store itself, papering over the windows. In 1948 he made his second and final move within the same building, this time to a large upstairs room which would be his haven for the rest of his life. [28]

Bryna began to be sick. As Sylvia remembers:

> She suffered from rheumatoid arthritis, which made her unable to do things. She stayed in bed, surrounded by Yiddish newspapers and books. She liked to settle down there and would call me beside her and read me articles and stories. When friends came, or my uncle Nachman, she

entertained them from the bedroom. She put on a dark shawl. [29]

This was the Depression, and a glimpse into almost any immigrant home of the period would have shown the harshness of the economic reality. Pieces of furniture rarely matched, and sheets were often made from bleached sugar-sacks. But the poverty of the Bercovitch home was noteworthy even in a community where hardship was the expected lot. Rose Mamelak Johnstone, daughter of the *Kanader Adler* writer Yakov Mamelak, often accompanied her father on his visits to the Bercovitch family in the mid-thirties. She remembers the flat vividly:

> We were all poor, but the Bercovitch poverty was special. My father sold newspapers until he found work as a machinist in 1939 — his writing was a passion, but not a living — but we always had enough to eat and we were well-clothed. The Bercovitch family had that terrible kind of poverty where clothes and food seemed inadequate. The atmosphere was emotionally charged, and Bercovitch and his wife seemed at daggers drawn. Perhaps it was because they had less money, fewer clothes, than anyone. [30]

There were broken pipes across the ceiling, and an old, cracked, black leather couch (called a "lunch") in one corner, and there was never enough to eat. But the fissured walls were covered with paintings, and the flat was full, not only of poverty and tension, but of books and newspapers and conversation and a passionate interest in the world outside. Visitors came every hour of the day, and they always lingered.

It was the poorest and yet the richest and most fascinating of homes.

1. *The History of the Montreal YM-YWHA*, p. 10, is incorrect in giving the date of the first exhibition as 1936. All the students interviewed remember the first show as ending the first season in May 1935, and the date is confirmed in the Bercovitch files in the National Gallery (courtesy of Charles Hill).

2. Paul Duval, *Four Decades: the Canadian Group of Painters and their Contemporaries* (Toronto: Clarke-Irwin, 1972), p. 96.

3. Sue Boroff was a student at the Y. Assya, Katya, and Sonya Guttkind were three sisters from Kherson who visited the Bercovitch home regularly. On 30 March 1950, Assya wrote to Bercovitch from her New York City home in what was evidently a reply to his condolences on the death of her husband, Philip

Rubin. It is clear from the letter that she and Bercovitch had kept in touch over the years. (Author's files.)

4. Ernst Neumann, "Jewish Artists," *Canadian Jewish Year Book 1940-1941*, ed. Vladimir Grossman (Montreal: Woodward, 1940), p. 173.

5. Dr. Harold Segall, interviewed in Montreal, 18 January 1987.

6. See, inter alia, Charles Hill, *Canadian Painting in the Thirties*, p. 16, and Lita-Rose Betcherman, *The Swastika and the Maple Leaf: Fascist Movements in Canada in the Thirties* (Toronto: Fitzhenry & Whiteside, 1975), p. 143.

7. Betcherman, *The Swastika and the Maple Leaf,* pp. 10-11.

8. Ibid., p. 32. *Le Devoir* reached the point in 1937 where its editor, Georges Pelletier, called for the expulsion of all Jews from all lands other than Palestine.

9. Groulx in a letter to a friend, Mr. Lamoureux, in 1954. The whole letter is quoted in Victor Teboul, *Mythe et images du Juif au Québec* (Montréal: Éditions de Lagrave, 1977), pp. 173-174. The letter is a long reflection by Groulx on what he saw as "the dreadful effects of the Jews' innate desire for money at all costs." For a detailed examination of the insidious propaganda put out by Groulx in the thirties, usually under the pen-name Jacques Brassier, see Jacques Langlais and David Rome, *Juifs et québécois français* (Montréal: Fidès, 1986), pp. 154-167.

10. Esther Trépanier, interviewed in Montreal, 29 November 1986. See also Lamonde and Trépanier, *L'avènement de la modernité culturelle au Québec,* pp. 102-103.

11. Lamonde and Trépanier, *L'avènement,* p. 90. Clarence Gagnon shared Maillard's views.

12. Madeleine Boyer, interviewed in Montreal, 24 January 1987.

13. Ghitta Caiserman-Roth, interviewed in Montreal, 9 December 1986, is only one of many who knew both men well and who share this opinion of their speech habits.

14. Judith Borenstein, interviewed Montreal, 25 January 1987.

15. Ruth Pressman, interviewed in Montreal, 19 May 1987 and 5 June 1987.

16. See correspondence Bercovitch/ McCurry/ Massey in National Gallery Archives, Ottawa, beginning with Bercovitch's "thank-you" letter addressed to Mrs. Massey, 28 November 1935. Massey's purchase of a Bercovitch is mentioned in a letter from Sidney Carter to McCurry, 9 December 1935, in the same file. Carter's letter is a reply to one from McCurry dated 7 December 1935, in which McCurry speaks very favourably of Bercovitch's earlier work, but slightingly of the Gaspé paintings of the summer of that year. McCurry describes them as "ordinary", but offers no explanation of his poor opinion.

17. Girard, "L'art," *Le Canada,* 30 October 1935. Girard's horror did not last long. In his *Le Canada* review, 20 August 1937, of Bercovitch's Gaspé paintings at W. Scott & Sons, he would call Bercovitch "un magnifique poète et tel que nous n'en avons peut-être jamais eu à Montréal" (a magnificent poet, such, perhaps, as we have never before known in Montreal).

18. "Reynald" (E.R. Bertrand), "Bercovitch n'a pas trahi Percé," *La Presse,* 2 November 1935.

19. Hill, *Canadian Painting in the Thirties,* p. 130.

20. Information from Ruth Pressman, who knew Fanny Lazar well. After the death of Fanny Lazar's husband, she and Bill Downes bought a cottage near Lac St. Charles, just outside of Québec City, where they were married. Pressman interview, 19 May 1987.

21. For details of the 1935 production, *Die Chappers,* and of other productions of the period, I am indebted to Gedalia Schacter, interviewed in Montreal, 2 April 1987.

22. Leiveck's *Die Oreme Meluche* was directed by Sigmund Lev and was presented at the Monument National Theatre under the auspices of the Jewish National Workers' Alliance. It was during the rehearsals for this play that Bercovitch met Solomon Ary who in 1940 would marry his daughter Sylvia. Ary, who had come from Bialystok in 1930, was a housepainter with no formal education who was desperate to understand and to participate in the artistic world. He began by mixing colours for Bercovitch's set. Later, he both acted and directed in Jewish theatre in Montreal. In 1976, at the age of 65, Ary began to set down his reminiscences and became a successful writer of short stories. (Conversations by the author with Solomon Ary, Montreal, January-August, 1987.)

23. *Winterset* by Maxwell Anderson was a production of The Little Theatre of the Y, and its stars were Sally Allister as Miriamne and Howard Schwartz as Mio. One of the "urchins" was William Shatner, in what was probably his first stage appearance.

24. *Der Oytzer* was the Communist Party's production for 1939.

25. Interview with Louis Muhlstock, Montreal, 27 November 1986.

26. Recollection of Sylvia B. Ary.

27. This 1937 incident, reported to the author by Solomon Ary, who helped Moishe Leib to compose his own death-notice, was only one of several such practical jokes. On one occasion, Moishe Leib feigned death to avoid his creditors. They insisted on coming into his room to prod the body, but he carried off the deception. Later, when he was in a position to repay, he upbraided them for their lack of lamentation over his corpse.

28. His studio address was given variously as 76, 78, or 80 Prince Arthur East. The choice seems to have been arbitrary and bore no relation to which part of the building he was using at the time. The building is now wholly occupied by the restaurant Bal St. Louis. The date of the second move within the building, to the larger upstairs room, is given as November 1948 in a letter to Bercovitch from his friend Félix-Xavier Chouinard, dated 16 November 1948, which discusses the move. (Author's files)

29. Recollection of Sylvia B. Ary.

30. Rose Mamelak Johnstone, interviewed in Montreal, 22 July 1987.

Plate 34.
From the collection of
Jack J. Gordon

"Mount Royal in Fall" c. 1948
oil on cloth
56 x 72 cm.

Plate 35.
From the collection of
Mr. & Mrs. Saul Shapiro

"Two Brothers" 1949
oil on canvas
86 x 78 cm.

CHAPTER SEVEN

Bercovitch and John Lyman: 1937-1942

It was in February 1937 that Bercovitch joined forces for the first time with the painter and art critic John Lyman.

Lyman, born in Maine but brought up in Montreal, had been so savaged by the critics at his first one-man show in 1913 that he had taken his Fauvist canvases and gone into exile in Paris for the next eighteen years.[1] In 1931 he returned permanently to Montreal to begin his struggle against what he perceived as Canadian parochialism. He was opposed not only to the Canadian Group, but to the rigid attitudes of the Royal Canadian Academy. His arch-enemy was the Academy's frequent spokesman, Dyonnet's friend Clarence Gagnon, who in 1939 lashed out at "the immense joke of modern art, a clever hoax engineered by greedy dealers."[2] Gagnon agreed with Charles Maillard of the Ecole des Beaux-Arts that modernism in art was the invention of Jews and Bolsheviks.[3] The Academy, like the Toronto-based Canadian Group, had powerful supporters, but Lyman's position was much strengthened when he was made art critic of *The Montrealer* in March 1936.[4] By January 1937 he was ready for his first major offensive.

Lyman spoke first to Bercovitch and to Brandtner, both of whom, like himself, had a European training. The three of them then approached eight others whose work, they felt, showed an openness to modern European influences. They were Prudence Heward, Jack Humphrey, Mabel Lockerby, Jean Palardy, Goodridge Roberts, Sarah Robertson, Marian Scott, and Jori Smith. None was an Academy member or supporter, and, unlike the Canadian Group of Painters, they shared no commitment to a single theme. As Robert Ayre said of them, what they had in common was

> a devotion to painting for its own sake, a personal and unacademic approach, and, at the same time, a tendency to sobriety rather than exuberance.[5]

Lyman arranged a show for the eleven in the Montreal Arts Club in February 1937, but it was still not clear either to Lyman or to Bercovitch how to assert themselves as an organized force in opposition to the Canadian Group and to the Academy. It was not until February 1938, a full year later, that they even decided to give their group a name, the Eastern Group. Ayre continues:

> This informal fellowship [with] no officers and few rules [was] drawn together not by a programme but by sympathy and agreement on the fundamentals of art, and because they thought it would be better to hold joint exhibitions than for each individual to aspire to a one-man show every year.[6]

By this time, only five of the original eleven were still involved; Bercovitch, Lyman, Goodridge Roberts, Jori Smith, and Jack Humphrey (a Maritimer who would be replaced by Philip Surrey in 1939). A sixth member, Eric Goldberg, was a newcomer.

Plate 36.
From the collection of
Harold B. Gordon

"Harold Gordon" 1949
pastel on paper
68 x 55 cm.

Plate 37.
From the collection of
Pinnie & Jack Gordon

"Street in Québec City" c. 1950
pastel on paper
39 x 58 cm.

Goldberg had known Lyman at the Ecole des Beaux-Arts in Paris, and, like Bercovitch, had studied both at the Bezalel School in Jerusalem and in Germany under Lovis Corinth. [7] His work, however, was very different from that of Bercovitch. Goldberg painted the joy he saw around him, and his paintings, in a style reminiscent of Dufy, are both light and charming.

The six held their first show as the Eastern Group in November 1938 at the Montreal gallery of W. Scott & Sons. The work shown was varied both in theme and style. They were all "extremely individualistic... not busy about being of their own time, or following any line, [be it] self-conscious regionalism, formalized pattern, or social comment." [8]

It would thus be an error to see the Canadian art world of the late 1930's as no more than two opposed monoliths, a Montreal-Toronto face-off, Man versus Nature, internationalism against parochialism. Both groups were more complex in their aims than some of their partisans would suggest. A.Y. Jackson did justice to neither group when he said, repeatedly, that "the chief difference between the two groups is that we [the Canadian Group] have roots in the soil and they [the Eastern Group] have not." [9] There was dissension even within the Canadian Group, and there were many in Canada, like André Biéler or the young Alfred Pinsky, who looked for leadership neither to Toronto nor to Montreal, but to the Social Realists of Mexico and the U.S.A. [10]

The Eastern Group's second exhibition took place in January 1940 at the Art Association of Montreal, but by this time Lyman had created an even more effective forum, the Contemporary Arts Society. (The Eastern Group would hold three more exhibitions, in 1942, 1945, and 1950, but it had yielded preeminence to the C.A.S. Unlike Lyman, neither Bercovitch nor Brandtner would hold dual membership for long, Brandtner resigning from the C.A.S. in 1940, [11] and Bercovitch from the Eastern Group in 1941. [12])

The Contemporary Arts Society was born at a meeting in Lyman's Montreal apartment in January 1939, when Lyman and Bercovitch and ten others decided to form a group which would include representatives of Québec's French-speaking majority. By May 1939, after advertising in both *The Standard* and *Le Jour,* they had twenty-six artist members, including five who were French. There was still a linguistic imbalance, but they thought that the unopposed election of Paul-Emile Borduas as Vice-President would attract more French members later. [13] (In this, they were correct. By January 1948, twenty-five of the forty-six artist members were French-speaking. [14] The increase in French membership was due not only to the popularity of Borduas and Pellan, but, indirectly, to World War II. As Graham McInnes points out, "after the fall of France in 1940, Montreal, along with Rio de Janeiro, became for some time the leading centre of publication in the French language." [15] This gave a tremendous impetus to French involvement in all the arts.)

The aims of the C.A.S. were made clear in Article 2 of its constitution:

> The objects of the Society shall be to give support to contemporary trends in art and to further the artistic interests of its members. [16]

The restrictions on membership were equally unambiguous. Article 3 offered a welcome in the Society only to those "who are neither associated with, nor partial to, any Academy." [17]

The first exhibition organized by the C.A.S. was a masterstroke. Instead of showing work by the Society's own members, the C.A.S. was able to borrow enough work from local collectors to put together a show devoted entirely to non-Canadian art. Called "Art of our Day", the May 1939 exhibition featured Derain, Dufy, Kandinsky, and Modigliani, and was an enormous critical success. [18] It signalled "the beginnings of a united effort for contemporary art and the invasion of the conservative halls of the Art Association." [19]

In December of the same year, the C.A.S. members exhibited their own work at the Stephens Gallery in Montreal, and again in December of 1940, this time at the galleries of the Art Association itself. It was a significant victory over the forces of reaction and Bercovitch had played a prominent role in the events leading up to it. Even if Lyman overshadowed him in the C.A.S. itself, few artists were more respected in Montreal, and none was his senior in the Jewish artistic community. As the art-historian Barry Lord comments:

> Rita Briansky studied during the Second World War years under Alexandre Bercovitch, the leading painter of the Jewish community. She was part of a circle around Bercovitch that included Ernst Neumann... and Louis Muhlstock. [20]

A number of critics have noted that Bercovitch's work of the period embraced more than one style. [21] He was painting nudes with gentle, sensual exaggeration, as in "Untitled Nude" (pastel 1942 — see Plate 29), and Canadian winter landscapes "which emphasize the contrast between the frigid white of the snow... and the harsh blues of the sky,"[22] like the "Laurentian Snow Scene" (oil c. 1938 — see Plate 24). He was painting children with "the strangely wistful, self-absorbed expression to be found on young faces,"[23] and, in so doing, was creating the kind of delightful character study found in "The Two Gangsters" (oil 1940 — see Plate 27), in which Bercovitch captures a thoughtful moment in the play of his son, Sacvan (on the right in the painting). For much of the work of the period, he was still using the familiar, confident divided brushstroke, as in "Two Huts on Beach near Percé" (oil 1937 — see Plate 21), but he was experimenting more than ever. "Montreal Street" (gouache c. 1939 — see Plate 25), for example, has a strange, dream-like quality that is rare in his work.

Sometimes, to achieve the effect of force and spontaneity, Bercovitch worked at great speed, and occasionally, as with "Gaspé: Cliff and Sea" (water-colour c. 1940 — see Plate 28), the freedom of the palette comes perilously close to disorder, but, as Neumann observed, "Bercovitch's failures are often more interesting than the successes of most of his contemporaries."[24]

Bercovitch found friends and even followers not only in Montreal but during his summers in the Gaspé Peninsula. He met Allan Harrison there in 1938, and the two men maintained a close relationship and an admiration for each other's work which was interrupted only when Harrison left to work in Rio de Janeiro in 1946. Harrison, a painter whose work is characterized by subtle understatement, re-calls that he and Bercovitch had "walked, talked, and laughed together very often during the summers at Percé," but had seen each other only rarely in Montreal, and then usually in the company of others at meetings of the C.A.S. (Harrison became Secretary of the C.A.S. in 1940, replacing Fritz Brandtner.)[25]

In 1941 Bercovitch met the usually reclusive Marc-Aurèle Fortin at Percé,[26] and he and the French-Canadian landscape painter found a friendship that would last through several summers. Writing to Louis Lange at the gallery L'art français, Fortin said, "Bercovitch does very beautiful work,"[27] and he told his biographer, Jean-Pierre Bonneville, in 1967 that he and Bercovitch had made three or four trips together along the Gaspé coast in the early forties.[28] There is no evidence, however, that the style of either artist had any lasting influence on the work of the other.

Sam Borenstein, who desperately wanted Bercovitch's friendship and good opinion, spent two summers in the Gaspé in 1942 and 1943 only because Bercovitch was there.[29]

If one were to judge by the opinions of his peers, Bercovitch by 1942 was at the pinnacle of his Canadian career. He was an intimate of Lyman and a founding member of the increasingly influential Contemporary Arts Society. (The internal bickering that was to destroy the Society was still some years away.[30]) Bercovitch was respected by his fellow-artists and adored by his students.

But, even while his art was receiving the approval of his peers, the rest of his life lay about him in ruins.

He was in a constant state of penury. In spite of critical acclaim, he made few sales, and even these were usually paid out over weeks and months. In 1942, his friends Ethel and Joe Achtman bought a Gaspé scene for fifty dollars and paid it out at a dollar a week. To celebrate the fiftieth payment, the Achtmans invited Bercovitch to dinner. Bercovitch told his hosts that he had had a similar arrangement with an American doctor, Selman Waksman, who had bought a Bercovitch landscape while on vacation in Percé. Waksman (who in 1943 discovered strepto-mycin) had made his payments by mail.[31]

As often as he could, Bercovitch resorted to barter. He paid his doctor and his landlord with paintings, and for items as unlikely as a toaster with paintings.[32] In 1942 he even secured a second-hand bicycle for Ninel with paintings although the bicycle was sold soon afterwards.[33] During the summers at Percé, at least during the period 1936 to 1939, he paid for his meals with paintings.[34]

He was trapped by his poverty. His work was prominent in all the major exhibitions, but it was common knowledge that both his house and his studio were always full of long-overdue bills, and that he had no choice but to accept almost any offer on his work.[35]

Every plan he devised to save the situation was doomed to failure. In the summer of 1937, he had gone to his beloved Percé with his daughter Sylvia and one of his Y students, Howard Daum. The trip, paid for by Daum's mother, was a success, and, fifty years later, Daum would feel able to say, "When I think of Percé, I wish that time could stand still and that 1937 would again materialize."[36] Sylvia, only fourteen at the time, remembers complaining to her father that Percé offered little to do in the evening. "But look at the sea," said Bercovitch in amazement. Sylvia did as she was told and sat with her father on the verandah of the boarding-house. For hour after hour, evening after evening, she watched the rhythm of the waves. "He was right," she says, "it was enough."[37]

After his experiment with the two young people, Bercovitch thought that he might be able to open a successful summer art school in the Gaspé, either at Percé or on Bonaventure Island. All he needed was finance. He approached one potential sponsor after another but was always refused.[38] After the summer of 1938, he did not speak about a school again.

Regina Shoolman, the friend and former social worker who had left Montreal for New York City, encouraged him to dream. As she says:

> Bercovitch came to New York in 1938. Charles and I had suggested he bring a portfolio and try for a Guggenheim Fellowship so that he could work in a warmer climate, California or Arizona. We put him up. The jury found him not really a Canadian and no longer a European. And anyway, Canadian and American art was not saleable.[39]

After this disappointment, Bercovitch began to talk instead about a New York show, but he spoke without conviction. Nothing in his North American experience suggested to him that he would ever make a living from his art. Rose Millman, the founder of Montreal's Dominion Gallery, who admired Bercovitch's paintings, was having little success in selling for him. When she put three of his works into the gallery window, three separate passers-by came into the gallery to ask that the "modern monstrosities" be removed from public view. (The three works were a portrait (see Plate 2), a seascape, and a street scene.)[40]

He grew more and more bitter as the truth became clear; he was fifty years old and there would never be a summer art school, or a Fellowship, or a New York exhibition.

In his pain, he turned his anger against his family. He and Bryna had long lived in a state of armed truce, with occasional skirmishes, but now he developed a new resentment, this time against his older daughter, Sylvia. A pupil of Anne Savage at Baron Byng High School, she was also studying with Fritz Brandtner at Bethune's Children's Art Centre (and would later take classes with Edwin Holgate at the Art Association).[41] She was displaying remarkable promise, and Bercovitch would often boast of her accomplishments to his friends,[42] but he could neither teach her himself nor pay her a direct compliment. When, in 1937, she won a Canada-wide painting contest, he refused to allow her to accept the prize, a visit to the International Exhibition in Paris. (Nor did he permit his son, Sacvan, to accept the summer art-school scholarship awarded by his primary school in 1942.)

It is possible that Bercovitch did not want his children, particularly Sylvia, to commit themselves to the artistic life, with its concomitant hardship. It may have been that he was jealous of another talent, or that he saw Sylvia increasingly as Bryna's ally. Whatever the reason, the estrangement between Bercovitch and Sylvia became total in 1940 when she married Solomon Ary, an unemployed housepainter and Bercovitch's sometime friend in the little world of Montreal's Yiddish theatre.

Bryna had joined her husband in opposing the match, and the confrontation between the parents on one hand, and Sylvia and Ary on the other, had been marked by angry ultimatums on both sides, and by at least one physical attack by Bercovitch on his prospective son-in-law.

In spite of the threats, Sylvia defied her father and the marriage took place on December 15, 1940. Bercovitch declared it to be an act of self-excommunication and forbade the family to have any further contact with her.

Bryna found the loss of her daughter increasingly hard to accept, and, when her first grandchild was born on May 24, 1942, the separation and loneliness became unbearable. Her marriage had long before shrivelled into hostility and silence. Bercovitch, when he came home, confined himself to a small room in the flat where he surrounded himself with untidy piles of his books and art materials. When Bryna made her furtive visits to Sylvia, it was to complain bitterly of the misery of her lot. When Ary, her son-in-law, offered to come to St. Dominique Street with Sylvia and the baby, and to take over the management of the household, Bryna said not only that Bercovitch would leave, but that he would be glad to go.

In the summer of 1942, Bryna made a formal request to Sylvia to return, with her husband and her child, to the house on St. Dominique Street. Bercovitch acted as they had all expected and, in September of the same year, he left the family. He put a cot in his Prince Arthur Street studio, and he never spoke to his wife or to Sylvia again.

1. Lyman broke his exile only once, in 1927, to return to Montreal for a successful one-man show at the Johnson Gallery. See Christopher Varley, *The Contemporary Arts Society* (Edmonton : Edmonton Art Gallery, 1980), p. 6.

2. Ibid., p. 2, and Guy Robert, *La peinture au Québec depuis ses origines* (Ste. Adèle, Qué. : Iconia, 1978), p. 82. Gagnon's April 1939 outburst was delivered to the Pen and Pencil Club of Montreal, but he repeated the sentiment on many occasions.

3. Lamonde and Trépanier, *L'avènement de la modernité culturelle au Québec,* p. 90.

4. Lyman remained art critic of *The Montrealer* until 1940, by which time he had launched the Contemporary Arts Society, a better vehicle for his proselytizing. See Dennis Reid, *A Concise History of Canadian Painting* (Toronto : Oxford U.P., 1973), p. 203.

5. Robert Ayre, "The Eastern Group Has a Show," *Saturday Night,* 17 December 1938, p. 36.

6. Ibid.

7. Goldberg both studied and taught at Bezalel. He knew Corinth not in Munich but in Berlin. During his years in Paris, 1906-1910, Goldberg was encouraged by Auguste Renoir. Author's interview with Regina Seiden Goldberg, Montreal, 10 May 1987. See also Colin S. MacDonald, *A Dictionary of Canadian Artists* (Ottawa : Canadian Paperbacks, 1967), p. 287.

8. Reid, *A Concise History,* p. 204.

9. Ibid.

10. Author in conversation with Alfred Pinsky, 5 February 1987. See also Charles Hill, *Canadian Painting in the Thirties,* p. 115. Biéler called the 1941 Kingston Conference to discuss precisely that problem, the need, as he saw it, for Canadian artists to make a political commitment. (Biéler also refused Lyman's invitation to join the C.A.S.)

11. Varley, *The Contemporary Arts Society,* p. 12. Philip Surrey says that Brandtner was less activist than Lyman and wanted the C.A.S. to be no more than an exhibiting society. See Lise Perrault — Surrey interview 28 March 1973. Interviews with Surrey, Paul Dumas, and Allan Harrison formed part of Perrault's graduate work under the direction of François-Marc Gagnon. (Files of Art History Department, Université de Montréal.)

12. Information supplied by Bercovitch to National Gallery Archives, Ottawa, 16 June 1942. Regina Seiden Goldberg, interviewed 10 May 1987, says that Bercovitch was very unhappy with the way his work had been hung at the Eastern Group's second show. She saw him remove his paintings from the wall in a rage.

13. Varley, *The Contemporary Arts Society,* pp. 6-12. See also Hill, *Canadian Painting in the Thirties,* p. 131. The slate was : Lyman — President, Borduas — Vice-President, Surrey — Treasurer, and Brandtner — Secretary. (Allan Harrison would replace Brandtner as Secretary within the year.)

14. Reid, *A Concise History,* p. 211.

15. Graham McInnes, *Canadian Art* (Toronto : McMillan, 1950), p. 78.

16. The Constitution of the C.A.S., reprinted in Varley, *The Contemporary Arts Society,* p. 38.

17. Ibid.

18. See, inter alia, Ayre, " 'Art of Our Day' Attracting Attention by its Vigour in Design," *The Standard,* 20 May 1939.

19. Hill, *Canadian Painting in the Thirties,* p. 132.

20. Barry Lord, *History of Painting in Canada* (Toronto : N.C. Press, 1974), p. 202. It is possible that Louis Muhlstock would not agree with Lord's description of the 1940 situation.

21. See Hill, *Canadian Painting in the Thirties,* p. 130 ; Ayre, "The Eastern Group Has a Show," *Saturday Night,* 17 December 1938, p. 36 ; and Ernst Neumann, "Jewish Artists," *Canadian Jewish Year Book 1940-41,* ed. Vladimir Grossman (Montreal : Woodward, 1940), p. 173.

22. Neumann, "Jewish Artists," p. 173.

23. Ibid.

24. Ibid.

25. Author's interview with Allan Harrison, Montreal, 1 December 1986. Harrison was Art Director for J. Walter Thompson Inc. in Montreal from 1939 to 1946, when he left to work for the same company in Rio de Janeiro. From 1948 to 1950 he painted in Paris and Italy. He then went to New York until he returned to Montreal in 1957. His mother wrote in 1951 to tell him of Bercovitch's death.

26. "Fortin painted in the mountains of the Gaspé as early as 1923, but he did not paint in Percé until 1941 when he met Bercovitch there :" René Buisson, President and Founder of the Marc-Aurèle Fortin Museum in Montreal, in conversation with the author, 6 January 1987, at the Museum. (Buisson befriended Fortin in his last years, arranging for his care in a residence.)

27. Letter on display at the Marc-Aurèle Fortin Museum, Montreal.

28. "Un jour d'août, 1967, l'interrogeant sur son travail en Gaspésie, il m'avait répondu, 'J'ai fait trois ou quatre voyages en Gaspésie avec Bercovitch. Bercovitch était un homme qui souffrait de la fièvre des foins. C'était un homme qui mangeait trop. Il était gros comme un tonneau. On a peint ensemble à Percé, à Port-Daniel, à Newport, à l'Anse-à-Beaufils, et dans d'autres villages" (One day in August 1967 I asked about his work in the Gaspé and he answered me, 'I took three or four trips in the Gaspé with Bercovitch. Bercovitch suffered from hayfever. He was a man who ate too much. He was as fat as a barrel. We painted together at... etc.' — author's transl.) : Jean-Pierre Bonneville, *Marc-Aurèle Fortin en Gaspésie* (Montréal : Stanké, 1980), p. 25. There is also a reference to Bercovitch joining Fortin at Newport in a letter written by Fortin to Louis Lange, 4 June 1942, and reprinted in Guy Robert, *Marc-Aurèle Fortin : l'oeuvre et l'homme* (Montréal : éditions France-Amérique, 1982), p. 191.

29. Kuhns and Rosshandler, *Sam Borenstein,* p. 50, seem to have made a mistake in giving the dates of the two Gaspé visits as 1945 and 1946. Judith Borenstein, interviewed in Montreal 25 January 1987, is sure of 1942 and 1943.

30. The collapse of the C.A.S. was the result of the rivalry between Alfred Pellan and Paul-Emile Borduas. Varley, *The Contemporary Arts Society,* p. 3, suggests that, while Borduas was committed to absolute liberation from artistic conventions, Pellan "tended to tinker with, rather than seriously question those conventions." Philip Surrey, interviewed by Lise Perrault 28 March 1973, emphasizes the discord between the disciples of Borduas, "les sagittaires", and the followers of Pellan, later called the "Prisme d'Yeux". Paul Dumas, interviewed by Lise Perrault 26 March 1973, believes that the ideological split between Borduas and Pellan was intensified when Pellan was offered a teaching job at the Ecole des Beaux-Arts by Maillard in June 1943. It was the job that Borduas had always wanted.

All sources agree with Reid, *A Concise History,* p. 217, on the sequence of events. Borduas, who had just published his "Refus

Global", defeated Lyman for the presidency of the C.A.S. at the meeting of 18 November 1948. Lyman would not then support Borduas against Pellan, who was withdrawing. Borduas resigned, and Lyman called for the dissolution of the C.A.S. Allan Harrison, in conversation with the author, 1 December 1986, and in an interview with Lise Perrault, 22 March 1973, takes the view that Borduas began his politicking as early as 1945 when he opposed the membership of candidates proposed by Harrison and Goodridge Roberts. "Borduas was inflexible: he could see nothing but abstract art," Harrison to author. (All sources agree that language was never a divisive issue, although both Pellan and Borduas spoke no English, and French-speakers were in a minority for most of the C.A.S.'s existence.)

31. Ethel Achtman, interviewed in Montreal, 18 April 1987.

32. Ibid. Ethel Achtman's late husband, Joe Achtman, was the manager of People's Store in Montreal in 1942.

33. Abe Gordon, interviewed in Montreal, 11 August 1987, remembers how Bercovitch came into his appliance and bicycle store on St. Lawrence in 1942. Bercovitch offered him a landscape and a portrait of Gordon's two daughters for a used children's bicycle. The offer was accepted.

34. Bercovitch made such an arrangement with Minnie Shapiro, a Montrealer whom he had met in the theatre group at "62 Rachel". Mrs. Shapiro operated a summer-only restaurant in Percé from 1936 to 1939. (Her son, Dr. Bernard Shapiro, in conversation with the author, 22 May 1987.)

35. Jack J. Gordon, interviewed in Montreal 27 November 1986. "While I painted with Bercovitch in his studio, people would come in, see the bills on the table, and offer twenty or thirty dollars for a masterpiece."

36. Letter to the author, 16 May 1987.

37. Recollection of Sylvia B. Ary.

38. In a letter dated 10 January 1938, one New Jersey doctor, a regular summer visitor to Percé, refuses Bercovitch's request for assistance with the project, which they evidently had discussed together at length, by pleading poverty. (Author's files.)

39. In conversation with the author, 11 December 1986. The New York City gallery Regina Shoolman would open with her husband, Charles Slatkin, would sell only European work.

40. The incident took place in 1941, according to Rose Millman's daughter, Bea Bazar, interviewed in Montreal, 6 February 1987.

41. In 1937 and 1938, Sylvia studied with Brandtner at the Children's Art Centre in Bethune's apartment on Beaver Hall Square. Bethune had left both the Centre and the apartment in Brandtner's care when he left for Spain. In 1939 and 1940, Sylvia studied with Edwin Holgate at the Art Association of Montreal.

42. Among others, Ruth Pressman, interviewed 19 May 1987 and 5 June 1987.

CHAPTER EIGHT

1942-1951: Camille

Bercovitch's decision to leave his wife and family in September was facilitated by events that had taken place in Percé several months earlier. In June he had met the woman who would be his companion and protectress for the rest of his life.

Camille de Guise was born on the Ile d'Orléans in 1897. An income from the family bookstore freed her from the necessity of working for a living and, when she met Bercovitch in 1942, she was well-travelled, passionately interested in the arts, and fluently bilingual. She had, as she put it, "not much, but enough to travel and to help my friends."[1] There had been a brief marriage, to Anton Swartz, a Norwegian businessman, but they had separated in 1940. A fervent Catholic, Camille never sought a divorce. As she said in 1986, "he may still be alive and I may still be married." In 1941, Camille met a young Toronto woman, Aimée Hoxie, who was spending a vacation looking for semi-precious stones along the Gaspé coast. Camille and Aimée, who dreamed of being a writer, became lifelong friends and travelling companions. In June of the following year, the circle was enlarged to include Bercovitch.

When Camille and Aimée first saw Bercovitch, he was deep in conversation with Marc-Aurèle Fortin. Later on the same day Camille saw him again, this time alone and painting on the shore. She approached him and they spoke. "There was an immediate affinity — 'un grand amitié'." The trio spent the rest of the summer together and, by the time Bercovitch was ready to return to Montreal at the end of August, Camille had made it clear to him that there would always be a place for him at Apartment 301 in the Chateau St. Louis in Québec City. It was also understood that his summers in the Gaspé would be subsidized. The promised financial help was not massive — "I would help him to sell and I would look after the food" — but it was enough to make Bercovitch feel secure. When Bryna told him that she had invited Sylvia and her family to share the St. Dominique Street flat, it was not difficult for Bercovitch to make the decision to leave. Camille's friendship offered him privilege without responsibility, in dramatic contrast, as he saw it, to the onerous family burden in Montreal. Camille wanted nothing from him except permission to look after him. Camille says:

> We were not romantically involved. We were free. He was free to do what he wanted. He could come and go as he wished. Sometimes I did not see him for months. When I saw him, I was like a secretary, someone who would plan... He lived in a dream-world: he was not in this world... He was a friend and an artist. I liked him and I felt that I had to help him in his work.

From 1942 until his death in 1951, Bercovitch would spend his summers in the Gaspé with Camille de Guise, often joined by Aimée Hoxie and sometimes by Marc-Aurèle Fortin, and his winters commuting between his Montreal studio and Camille's Québec City apartment. Only occasionally would he vary his routine, perhaps by a sketching party at Aimée's home in Toronto, or by a visit to the Bay of Fundy with Camille.

Through Camille, Bercovitch entered a whole new Catholic world. He was warmly received in particular by the Chouinard family in Québec City. Félix-Xavier Chouinard was the City Clerk of Québec City, a cousin through marriage of Anton Swartz, and a dedicated Russophile. Bercovitch became "Uncle Sasha" to Chouinard's daughters, Monique and Suzanne, and a kind of cultural idol to Chouinard himself. In a letter to Bercovitch dated November 16, 1948, Chouinard writes:

When I think of you, I think of that adorable friendship between King David (your dear self) and his humble friend Jonathan, the son of Saul... They depict exactly our own friendly relations since the first day I met you at Camille's... Your favourite authors are also mine... On the Russian steppe we gallop together in the same troika as if we were both created by Gogol in his marvellous *Dead Souls,* [2]

and, in another letter dated January 31, 1950:

What a great poet you are yourself, singing aloud the most ravishing pages of *Boris Godounov* with Moussorgsky's music, and reciting the adorable poems of Pushkin. [3]

Bercovitch also made many friends among the Catholic clergy. In 1944 at Percé, in the company of Camille and Fortin, he met Father Etienne Marion of the Seminary of Joliette. [4] Together with Father Wilfrid Corbeil, a distinguished painter and the founder of Joliette's Art Museum in 1942, Father Marion had made Joliette a centre of artistic endeavour in Québec. Father Marion, a man both joyful and outgoing, fell in love with Bercovitch's work and invited him to give an exhibition at the Seminary in the following year. During the preparations for the show, which finally took place in November and December of 1945, Father Marion became a frequent visitor to Camille's Québec City home, and Bercovitch came to know the whole of Joliette's religious community.

The community responded with enthusiasm to the exhibition. "Faced with so much beauty, one feels oneself to be in the presence of greatness,"* was the reaction of the Seminary's journal, [5] and Bercovitch, much moved, painted an icon which was accepted by Father Maurice Ouellet in the name of the community. At the Seminary's centennial celebration in 1947, Bercovitch and Camille were the honoured guests.

Bercovitch found a reception in Québec City and in Joliette that he had never enjoyed in Montreal. In addition to the group of friends centred on Camille and Father Marion, there were the Schulmans, John and David, the brothers of Regina Shoolman. They made Bercovitch and Camille welcome both at their Québec City homes and at their Lac Beauport country house. John Schulman's son David remembers how his parents kept a huge roll of brown wrapping paper just for Bercovitch's visits. [6] The artist would lower his considerable bulk on to the hard wooden floor, and, with one great sweep, would open the roll to the width of the apartment. Grunting and wheezing at every movement, with the two boys, David and Charles, kneeling beside him, he would create, in great expressive strokes, a whole menagerie of animals.

It is not surprising that, after 1942, Bercovitch began to spend less and less time in Montreal. He no longer submitted work to the Art Association for the Spring Show or to the Academy for the Fall Exhibition. (There was one exception, the portrait of the black girl, "The Negress," that hung in the 1950 Spring Show.) He kept his Montreal studio, however, and continued to give winter classes at the Y until 1946. He also continued to accept commissions for hotel and exhibition decoration, [7] and it was such a contract with the hotel Le Chalet that produced one of his masterpieces, "Petrushka," (oil on gold paint on canvas 1946 — see Plate 30).

In the autumn of 1946, after spending the summer with Camille at Percé, Bercovitch went to work at the hotel in the Laurentian resort of Ste. Agathe. Le Chalet had been opened in 1939 as a honeymoon hotel for Americans in the summer, recruited mainly by an agent on commission in New York, and as a centre of Yiddish culture for the rest of the year. Among its frequent guests were the Talmudist Menashe Ungar, the poet Yaakov Glatstein, the painter Fanny Mazel, and the writer Isaac Bashevis Singer. After the economies of the war years, the hotel was to be renovated, and Bercovitch was commissioned to produce a great mural for the bar. [8]

He went for his inspiration to two sources, the travelling puppet-shows of his Russian childhood, and Diaghilev's 1911 ballet, *Petrushka*. Petrushka was the Russian Punch who, after beating his wife and killing people, is dragged off to Hell by the Devil. For the 1911 ballet, Benois, who created the décor and libretto to accompany Stravinsky's score, eliminated the Devil but added new elements; a Magician who would bring Petrushka to life, a ballerina with whom

---

* "devant tant de beauté, on a la sensation d'être en présence de quelque chose de grand"

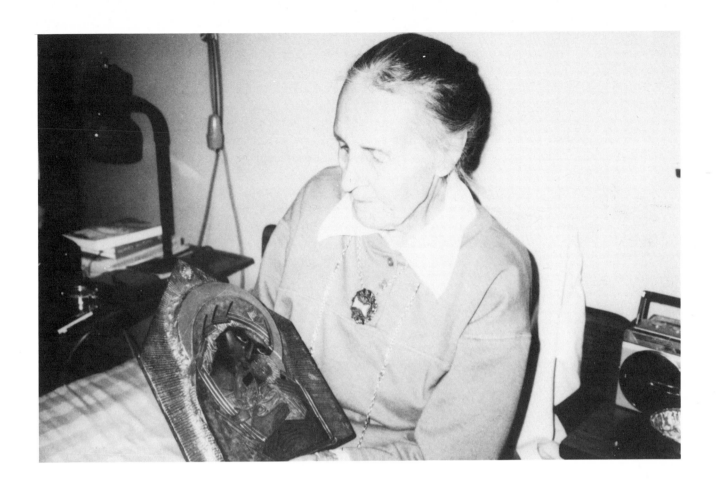

Top — An eighty-nine year-old Camille de Guise in Québec City, December 1986. She is holding a smoke-blackened ikon, the only work by Bercovitch remaining to her after a disastrous fire in her Chateau St. Louis apartment in 1980.

Photo by author

Bottom — "Father Etienne Marion c.s.v." (in front of the now-disappeared chapel of Gros-Morne in Gaspésie) by Alexander Bercovitch, 1944, pastel on paper, 60.3 x 45.3 cm. A gift of the abbé François Lanoue to the Musée d'art de Joliette. Father Marion became part of the circle around Camille de Guise.

Reproduced by courtesy of the Musée d'art de Joliette.

Petrushka would fall in love, and a "blackamoor" who would be both Petrushka's rival and his executioner. Benois also situated the action in the great Butter Week Fair, that festive period preceding Lent when booths and rides were set up in St. Petersburg in the square outside the Winter Palace.[9]

Bercovitch's mural incorporated all the elements of both sources, but there is no similarity between the frenzied Expressive gaiety of Bercovitch's work and the curiously static and painfully realistic fairground set of Benois' first act.[10] Bercovitch's "Petrushka" shows a Chagall-like disregard for conventions of time and space and compresses the whole narrative of both fable and ballet into one brilliantly animated scene. The Devil bestrides a booth and waves a balalaika as if directing the human comedy playing below. All the traditional figures of a Russian fairground are present; the stout coachmen with their mittens stuck in their belts, the strong man, the musicians, and the monkey; but they share the space with the figure of the top-hatted Magician with the dark and fair women, allegorical figures of Good and Evil, and with the death of Petrushka in the fantasy background. Paradoxically, all the faces are mask-like except that of Petrushka himself. In spite of his elongated nose, his face shows a bizarre and touching humanity as he sees death approach in the moment. The mural is a triumph of controlled delight in colour, from the oriental elaboration in the shawls of the foreground to the simplicity of the pale blue of Petrushka's last moment.

The patrons of Le Chalet would not enjoy the mural for too long. In 1949 it was taken down as part of yet another renovation. In the reconstructed bar there was no space for it, and it lay rolled up and walked on in a corner until rescued by the artist later in the same year. It then hung over his cot at the back of his studio until his death.[11]

After painting "Petrushka", Bercovitch returned to winter in Montreal where he never tired of the life and humour of the St. Lawrence Boulevard cafés. The humour often had a bitter edge but Bercovitch was usually an observer rather than a participant. Only on one occasion did Bercovitch himself play a part in a jest, a rather cruel one, and out of it came a fine portrait.

Among the habitués of Schwartz's Hebrew Delicatessen was a feeble-witted deliveryman, Moishele Geller,[12] who rejoiced in the delusion that he was a world-famous cantor. Nothing pleased him more than to sing for the customers, to the annoyance of the staff, or to describe in detail the ovation he had received at his most recent concert. Bercovitch decided one day to give Moishele Geller a

measure of immortality and invited him to sit at the Prince Arthur Street studio. The result was a portrait, "Moishele Geller, Cantor" (oil 1946 — see Plate 31), that would attract much critical attention. Robert Ayre said of it:

> Cantor Moishele Geller has no body under his shawl, but that may be symbolical; his face beneath the fez [sic], with its prominent nose and ears and its eyes, almost fanatic in their intentness, dominates the room,[13]

and Michael Forster commented that:

> The formal curve of the white shawl separates the expressionist head from the prismatic hand below, and the artist has even added collage in the Hebrew script, yet the whole picture is knit together by the richness of its colour.[14]

No one outside Bercovitch's circle knew the secret of the painting, or knew why the supposed cantor had a hand like Harlequin's. (Bercovitch's explanation of the hand to his friend Jack J. Gordon was that "it shows the joke. For a man of my talents to spend so much time on a crazy man is an irony, is humorous."[15])

During the long periods he spent away from Montreal, Bercovitch maintained a constant correspondence with his friends, often writing about the contentment he found with Camille in Québec City or the Gaspé.

Reuben Leaf the calligrapher replied from New York to one such letter:

> I was very happy to hear that... you have found at last the princess of your youthful dreams, 'La Princesse Lointaine' by Edmond Rostand, which you used to recite with your eyes fixed far, far away. So it seems that dreams can come true.[16]

Another friend, the sculptor Malchi, added his congratulations to Bercovitch as a postscript to a 1950 letter describing a Hadassah-organized art show which had not lived up to its promise. As Malchi put it:

> No one bought but everyone ran around like poisoned mice. The ladies made some fine speeches and so did the consul from Israel. They sang 'Hatikvah'. And so ended the evening. And our great artists left with

heads down and hopes gone. This could only happen in Montreal with her great Intelligentsia. I envy you that you are now in a quiet, peaceful district, far from people, far from tumult, and even farther from the Intelligentsia.[17]

One of the artists at the exhibition that Malchi describes was Eric Goldberg, a friend of Bercovitch from the days of the Eastern Group. In a cartoon he drew in his diary, the usually gentle Goldberg permitted himself a little barbed fun at the expense of the well-meaning ladies.

whole hierarchy of professional Intelligentsia has spread itself the length and breadth [of Montreal] and it's like being in Egypt under slavery. If I had somewhere to run away to, I'd do it, even if it were the grave.[18]

Bercovitch's friends were less pleased by his news that his work had changed in its subject matter. He had been influenced by Camille and her circle. Now there were more pastel portraits and flower arrangements and soft landscapes and even religious

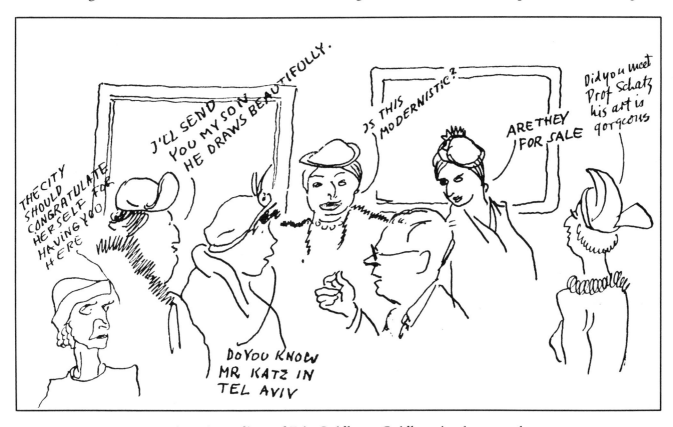

From the private diary of Eric Goldberg. Goldberg in glasses at the centre.
(Reprinted by permission of Regina Seiden Goldberg)

It was the great poet J.I. Segal who attacked most viciously what he perceived to be the philistinism of the Montreal community. A letter to Bercovitch in October 1947 is a cry from the heart:

> I'm more than envious of you that you finally got out of this local swamp and that you're artistically, spiritually, and even physically coming to yourself. Our Montreal today, especially our corner of it, is unbelievably empty, like a wasteland. The

studies. Reuben Leaf was very unambiguous in his disapproval of the new direction:

> With Madonnas you will be able, without doubt, to do good business. Should you also 'convert' a little, your business will really go well. What on earth do you find in these Madonnas? ... Jews with Madonna complexes have always revolted me.[19]

There was no conversion, but it seems clear that Bercovitch often painted that which would be pleasing to Camille. He was still, however, capable of very fine work, from Picasso-like experiment to lush nudes and rich landscapes and portraits (see Plates 32 to 37).

In spite of Bercovitch's claims to Reuben Leaf, to Malchi, and to Segal, there is much evidence that the last decade of his life, the period without Bryna, was not entirely happy. Rolland Boulanger, who painted with him in the summer of 1946 at Percé, remembers:

> He could be charming, even tender and sentimental, on occasion, but I was always left with the memory of a man going through what I might call a creative crisis, one which affected him a great deal. His moods varied, and, because I didn't know him well, I didn't know why, having been so friendly one day, he would be so nervous, even surly, the next... He sketched in situ, confidently, quickly, and with an ease of which I was secretly envious, and his big, bulging eyes took in everything. When he returned to his temporary studio to work from his sketches, the agonizing began the moment he entered. It was better to leave him then, before irascibility and even hostility and suspicion took over. [20]

There was much that might have been tormenting Bercovitch.

1. Camille de Guise, interviewed in Québec City, 26 November 1986. All subsequent remarks attributed to her are from this interview.

2. Chouinard to Bercovitch, 16 November 1948. Letter in author's files.

3. Ibid.

4. Much of the information concerning Bercovitch and the Seminary of Joliette was given to the author by the abbé François Lanoue c.s.v., interviewed in Joliette, 13 December 1986. Father Lanoue was a friend of Father Marion and Father Corbeil, and met Bercovitch several times.

5. Réal Aubin, "Une exposition des peintures d'Alexandre Bercovitch," *Le Séminaire de Joliette,* 10 (1945), p. 10.

6. David Schulman, interviewed in Montreal, 6 February 1987.

7. Bercovitch was not the only artist to undertake such commissions. Jori Smith and her husband, Jean Palardy, did similar commercial work in 1938. See Ayre, "Eastern Group Has a Show," *Saturday Night,* 17 December 1938, p. 36. In addition, the artist Henry Eveleigh, after he arrived from Shanghai in 1938, worked with Bercovitch on display backgrounds for several industrial exhibitions (Eveleigh in conversation with the author, 10 December 1986).

8. Le Chalet was administered by Abe and Leike Handelman, one of the four couples who owned it. For information concerning the hotel, I am indebted to Leike Handelman's sister, Ruth Pressman, interviewed in Montreal, 19 May and 5 June 1987.

9. Richard Buckle, *Diaghilev* (London: Hamish Hamilton, 1979), pp. 179-181, 196-203. Bercovitch was not the only Montreal artist to paint a "Petrushka". In 1937, Paraskeva Clark, also of Russian origin, painted a Futurist "Petrushka" in which a puppet policeman, encouraged by "The Capitalist", beats a fallen worker. See Hill, *Canadian Painting in the Thirties,* p. 95.

10. The Benois set is reproduced in Serge Lifar, *A History of the Russian Ballet,* transl. Arnold Haskell (London: Hutchison, 1954), p. 160 f.

11. "Petrushka" was seen above Bercovitch's bed many times by Jack J. Gordon, interviewed in Montreal, 27 November 1986 and 25 May 1987, who bought it from the artist's estate in 1956.

12. Moishele is the diminutive of Moishe. The account of the incident is given by Jack J. Gordon.

13. Robert Ayre, "Review of Fine Arts Museum Show," *Montreal Star,* 24 March 1951. Ayre confuses a fez with a yarmulke. It is not Ayre's only error. In "Bercovitch Exhibition is Hospitable," *Montreal Star,* 13 January 1951, he says, "Bercovitch had never had an exhibition of his own except one in Joliet [sic] several years ago." Joliette is incorrectly spelled, and Bercovitch had three solo exhibitions in Montreal in the 1930's.

14. Michael Forster, "A. Bercovitch, R. Watt Paintings at Museum," *The Standard,* 24 March 1951.

15. Jack J. Gordon interview, 25 May 1987.

16. Reuben Leaf to Bercovitch, 1 February 1947. Letter in author's files. Translated from Yiddish by Sylvia Ary.

17. Malchi to Bercovitch, 4 October 1950. Letter in author's files. Translated from Yiddish by Sylvia Ary.

18. Segal to Bercovitch, October 1947. Letter in author's files. Translated from Yiddish by Sylvia Ary.

19. Reuben Leaf to Bercovitch, 18 June 1947. Letter in author's files. Translated from Yiddish by Sylvia Ary.

20. Rolland Boulanger, "Départ... Alex. Bercovitch," *Arts et Pensée,* 2 (March, 1951), p. 52. Author's translation.

CHAPTER NINE

The Family

As he spent his days with Camille, whether in the Gaspé or at her Chateau St. Louis apartment or at the Ritz-Carlton Hotel, her home in Montreal when she visited,[1] Bercovitch could not have avoided reflecting on what had befallen his family.

After he left Bryna and the two younger children in September 1942, they were joined at 4264 St. Dominique Street by Sylvia, her infant daughter Rachel, and her husband, Solomon Ary. Although he was hard-pressed financially and could find house-painting work only occasionally, Ary assumed responsibility for the whole family. Bryna was able to contribute the twenty dollars a month that the *Kanader Adler* had begun to pay her for a regular column, and Ninel was seventeen and soon to move out to economic independence. The arrangement might have worked if it had not been for the nine year-old Sacvan. The issue of child-support for the boy became a test of strength between Bercovitch and his son-in-law. Neither of them could forget the emotions engendered by Bercovitch's opposition to Sylvia's marriage. A social worker from the Baron de Hirsch Institute, called in to arbitrate, fixed Bercovitch's weekly support for his son at five dollars. Inexplicably, the social worker and Ary also decided that Sacvan should collect the money himself. The nine year-old became not merely a pawn but the whole chess-board in the struggle between Bercovitch and Ary. Every Friday, hatless and glove-less in a cruel Montreal winter, the boy would hurry the several blocks between his home and his father's studio to ask for money. The few dollars assumed mythic proportions in the battle for supremacy between the two adult males and when, on one nightmarish Friday, Sacvan lost the money en route and Bercovitch refused to replace it, there was an explosion of emotion at both ends of the journey.

In the summer of 1943, Sacvan spent a month with his father at Fanny Lazar's rented cottage in the Laurentians, a month in which Bercovitch, busy painting, left his son alone all day and every day. After Bercovitch and the boy returned to Montreal and the struggle between Bercovitch and his son-in-law resumed, all parties agreed that it would be simpler if Sacvan were to live elsewhere, especially since Bryna's health was growing worse. The Baron de Hirsch Institute found a foster-home for Sacvan. He would spend the next five years in such homes, seeing his mother regularly but his father only occasionally. In 1946, Bercovitch, recuperating from a kidney operation,[2] spent two months with his son at one of the foster-homes.[3] Sacvan remembers that:

> I stayed out of the house except to sleep. It was not out of hate, but out of confusion as to what my appropriate response should be.[4]

After that summer of 1946, with the single exception of one, chance, wordless encounter on the street, Bercovitch did not see his son again.

Bercovitch must also have been aware, through Ninel, whom he saw from time to time, that Bryna's health, like his own, was deteriorating steadily. She was becoming crippled by rheumatoid arthritis, and her attempt in 1948 to set up a new, independent home for herself and Sacvan lasted only a few months. (In 1951, she would be admitted to the Hospital of Hope, Montreal's Jewish hospital for the incurably sick, where she would live until her death in 1956.)

Friends testify that Bercovitch wept over his son,[5] and that, forgetting Camille, he raged against Ary, whom he blamed for the disintegration of the family. One such scene took place at the Dominion Gallery in Montreal. The owner, Rose Millman, always kept open-house on Friday nights, and Bercovitch was a frequent visitor. One evening, after arguing with A.Y. Jackson about art, he began a denunciation of his son-in-law that was unusual only in its length and violence. It was a topic of which Bercovitch never tired.[6]

In 1950, his cup of bitterness overflowed. He had long been aware that his first wife and their son, Kalmushe, were still alive, having emigrated from Russia to Palestine in 1926. He and Baila had even received news of each other through Isa Kremer, a folk-singer whose tours took her to both Israel and Montreal, though Bercovitch confided this information only to a very few close friends.[7] He had permitted Bryna and the children to assume that the first family had perished in the famines of the thirties in the Ukraine.

In early 1950, Shloime Wiseman, principal-superintendent of the Montreal Yiddish Folk Shule, was attending a seminar in Israel. A fellow-teacher, Baila V'Dovetz from Haifa, asked him to deliver a letter to Alexander Bercovitch in Montreal.[8]

The letter contained the news of the death of Kalmushe. Kalman Barkov, as he was known, had fought for Israel during its struggle for independence, and had been deafened by a premature explosion while dynamiting a British installation. On August 19, 1949, while driving a tractor on his kibbutz, Givaot Zeid, he did not hear the malfunction of the engine and was crushed to death when the machine overturned. Baila included with the letter a little memorial book put out by Kalmushe's friends.[9]

Bercovitch was overcome by the news. He carried the little book, with its photographs of his dead son, on his person for the rest of his life. It was one of the few objects found in his pockets when he died. He was even prompted to make a few pathetic written overtures to his surviving son, Sacvan. One, dated May 14, 1950, was as follows:

Dear Son,

I want to see you and I beg that you should come to see me. Don't be bitter against me. Now you are old enough, you should come and let's make peace. I hope that you will understand. Don't put it off, and answer soon when you are coming. You know my address. With love, your father,

Alexander Bercovitch.[10]

But Bercovitch had damaged the relationship beyond the point of repair, and there was never an answer. Among his papers, after his death, his family found a poem in his own handwriting. Written in Yiddish, and clearly to a male because of the gender of the penultimate line, it reads in English as:

Autumn, the breadth of sadness
Over fields and woods,
There stretched the path
Of our destiny.
My dear one,
The leaves are falling.[11]

Photo — Sacvan Bercovitch in 1948 at the age of 15. (Author's files)

1. Mrs. Helen Maron, interviewed in Montreal, 12 May 1987, is a Montreal art collector who knew Bercovitch well in the period 1937 to 1944. She and her husband often had Bercovitch to dinner. She remembers that, after 1942, she and her husband would often give him a lift to the Ritz-Carlton Hotel where Camille would be waiting for him.

2. Mrs. Edith Gold, interviewed in Montreal, 3 February 1987, remembers how her late husband, Dr. Solomon Gold, would urge Bercovitch to take better care of himself, particularly after his hospitalization in 1946. Bercovitch had both heart and kidney problems, and was hospitalized for a second time in early 1950. The Bercovitch-Gold friendship was a close one, and the Gold's second son, Alexander, born in 1952, was named after Bercovitch.

3. Sacvan's foster-home in 1946 was with a Mrs. R. Goldberg. It was the home at which Sacvan spent three of his five years in foster-care.

4. Sacvan Bercovitch, in conversation with the author, 1987.

5. Among others, Mrs. Luba Chaitman, interviewed in Montreal, 19 April 1987, a childhood friend of Bercovitch from Kherson, and Mrs. Esther Handel, interviewed in Montreal, 20 May 1987. Mrs. Handel, with her late husband Harry, owned the Everyman Bookstore on Ste. Catherine Street until 1971. Bercovitch often dropped in at the bookstore in the period 1942 to 1945 and, very occasionally, came back to their apartment to eat. After a glass of wine, he always wept.

6. Florence Millman, interviewed at her West End Gallery in Montreal, 30 January 1987. The daughter-in-law of Rose Millman, she witnessed several such outbursts by Bercovitch at the Friday evening gatherings.

7. Mrs. Edith Gold, interviewed 3 February 1987, remembers that it was some years before the proclamation of the State of Israel in 1948 when her husband told her that Bercovitch had a son in Palestine. It was a confidence, and not to be discussed. Baila V'Dovetz told Sylvia Ary in Haifa in 1977 that Isa Kremer had given her and Bercovitch news of each other. (Interview in author's files.)

8. Mrs. Luba Chaitman, interviewed 19 April 1987, was told by Mr. Wiseman of his meeting with Baila. Wiseman, fearing to carry contraband, insisted that he be given the letter unsealed so that he might check the contents.

9. The date, place, and circumstances of Kalman Barkov's death are taken from this memorial book, as are the photographs of Baila V'Dovetz and her son. (Author's files)

10. Author's files. Translated from Yiddish by Sylvia Ary.

11. Author's files. Translated from Yiddish by Sylvia Ary.

Top — Alexander Bercovitch at the age of fifty-nine, shortly before his death.

Photo : author's files

Bottom — a poem by Bercovitch in Yiddish, found among his papers after his death (see Chapter Nine).

Author's files

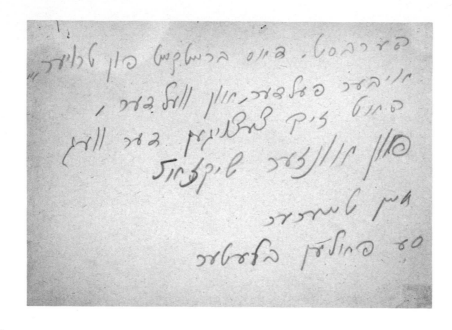

CHAPTER TEN

The Last Day:
January 7, 1951

As 1950 drew to a close, Bercovitch was occupied with the preparations for a retrospective, his first one-man show since Joliette in 1945. It was planned for January 1951 at the new YM-YWHA building on Westbury Avenue in Montreal.[1] Like his friends Malchi and J.I. Segal, Bercovitch had mixed feelings towards Montreal's Jewish community and had been particularly disappointed when so few had bothered to visit him in hospital in 1946 and again in early 1950.[2] Nevertheless, he had yielded to the plans of his wellwishers, including the always-devoted Moe Reinblatt, and had agreed to the exhibition. With the assistance of a new acolyte, Harold Gordon, Bercovitch was preparing nearly eighty of his works to hang in the three lounges of the new building, and trying to put some order into the chaos of canvases, paints, unwashed plates, brushes, bottles, and bedclothes that was his studio.[3]

The retrospective was to open at 7 p.m. on Sunday, January 7, 1951. The invited speakers included the doyen of Canadian art dealers, Dr. Max Stern,[4] and Dr. Solomon Gold, prominent in the community, one of the sponsors of the exhibition, and a long-time friend of Bercovitch. It was very rare for Dr. Stern to speak in public outside his own Dominion Gallery,[5] and his willingness to do so at Bercovitch's opening was a great compliment to the artist.

The evening before the opening was exhausting. Even with the help of young Harold Gordon, the overweight and obviously unwell Bercovitch found the physical effort of hanging his work almost more than he could bear. His heart was weak and all the

years of neglecting his diet and general health had caused irreparable damage to his kidneys. He had not long before come out of hospital, and he was weary from the many months of preparation for the show.

He slept late the next morning, but woke in time to go to see Mrs. Caiserman, the wife of his old friend and benefactor who had died two weeks earlier. He was anxious to offer his condolences, but he was tired after he climbed the steep steps to the Caiserman home on Maplewood Avenue, and he was pleased when Mrs. Caiserman asked him to stay for lunch. He left a little after 2 p.m., saying that he had a few errands to do before taking the streetcar to the exhibition, which still needed a few final touches.[6]

The narrative is best taken up at this point by Ruth Pressman, who attended the opening of the exhibition in the evening of the same day.

Philip [Pressman] and I arrived early. We came with Malchi and his wife, and with Chayele Grober. This was to be our friend's great evening. The speeches were supposed to begin at 7, but Bercovitch didn't arrive. By 9 o'clock, the comments, mostly in Yiddish or Russian, were very derogatory. 'He wouldn't bother to get a clean shirt.' 'He doesn't want to be an exhibit.' 'He doesn't want to face a Jewish crowd.' There were even jokes about the 'late' Mr. Bercovitch... At 9 o'clock, two hours after the scheduled time, the exhibition was opened, without speeches or fanfare... By 10:30 I began to be uneasy. I was angry with the criticism I overheard. I snapped at many, 'Couldn't you imagine that he might be sick?' My husband thought that I over-reacted, but I thought that the night was like a wedding ceremony and that the bridegroom hadn't arrived. Chayele asked to be taken home... After we dropped her off, I told my husband that we should check at Bercovitch's studio on Prince Arthur... We arrived at midnight. Malchi, his wife, and I waited in the car while Philip knocked. A door adjacent to the studio opened, and Bercovitch's neighbour told my husband that the police had been there... We went to the police-station, and the police confirmed that they had a man in the mortuary. He had the little memorial book for Kalmushe in his pocket, with a streetcar ticket and a visiting-card with the studio address. The card was in the old-fashioned Russian style, announcing 'Alexander Bercovitch — Artist'. The police had been to the studio, but, of course, had found no one there. Philip saw the body... We went home and phoned Sylvia. Ary and Sacvan went to make a formal identification.[7]

Bercovitch had suffered a massive heart-attack as he waited for his streetcar at 3 p.m. on the corner of Mount Royal Avenue and St. Lawrence Boulevard. He had died in the street. His body had lain unclaimed in the mortuary until the early hours of Monday morning when, ironically, it was his estranged son-in-law, summoned by the Pressmans, who came to assign the corpse an official identity. (Sacvan accompanied Ary to the mortuary but, at the last moment, turned back. Ary made the identification alone.)

The newspapers of the next few days all carried obituaries. Israel Rabinovitch of the *Kanader Adler* and the *Canadian Jewish Chronicle* published a front-page lament in both newspapers:

But a moment ago, there lived a man named Alexander Bercovitch... A grim and bitter and lonely life had he, wandering about us like a lost soul, a stranger... Just as reality for Bercovitch was dark, so were his paintings suffused with light; just as reality brooded over him in foreboding grey, so did his work, resplendent, shine forth in dream-like blue. He paid dearly, so dearly, for the luxury of bathing himself in this transcendent blueness. And they paid dearly too, whose fate was destined to be interwoven in his...[8]

Robert Ayre, in the *Montreal Star*, reflected on the man, the exhibition, and the artist:

He was not without friends and patrons, but he had no public recognition and of late his work had been infrequently seen. When he did not come to the opening on Sunday night, some of the people felt affronted, as if the guest of honour had spurned their advances. They remembered that he was an independent man, an eccentric, and they wondered if he had been embittered by solitude and neglect.

Others remembered that he was shy as a child, and concluded that, at the last minute, he couldn't face the limelight. His close friends... were puzzled by his absence. No one knew that he had died suddenly in the street a few hours before.

... At his best ... Bercovitch had a power and individuality that carried him beyond the orbit of popular taste, though he never lost the human touch. It is too early to assess his place in Canadian painting...[9]

Jean Dénéchaud, in *La Presse,* was generous in his assessment:

We knew Bercovitch to be a character, and we assumed his failure to attend his own show to be just another of his eccentricities... His premature death leaves behind the memory of a gifted artist, a sincere artist who painted only what he sincerely felt... This big, terribly simple man, whose bright eye caught every detail of our streets and modern life, was a leading light at the shows of the Fine Arts Museum, the Academy, the Eastern Group, and the Contemporary Arts Society. His canvases had something remarkable about them, and they placed Bercovitch... among those painters who were influencing the direction of Canadian painting.[10]

Rolland Boulanger, in *Arts et Pensée,* after much praise of Bercovitch the artist, pointed out the irony of his death:

After more than twenty years of work in Québec, he had not harvested the public recognition he deserved. He died at precisely the moment when we were getting ready to give it to him. [11]

His friend, the poet A.M. Klein, paid him moving tribute :

He will be remembered. He will be remembered, not only by his friends who will always recall his shy, his naif personality, his mosaic hesitations in speech, his inarticulate verbal descriptions, but by all lovers of art who will cherish before their eyes the uninhibited eloquence of his palette, the brightness he brought down from the sky, the hundreds of days wherein, like Joshua, he told the sun to stand still.

Honour to his memory ! Glory to his art ! [12]

There was much to remember. He had lived a turbulent personal life and had been part of great events on two continents. He had brought a superb European artistic training to Montreal and had taught a whole generation of Jewish artists while himself only barely surviving the bitterness of the Depression. He had played a key role in the evolution of modern art in Canada and, at his best, his work had been hailed as powerful and innovative. In the other obituaries in other newspapers and in other magazines, [13] and in the conversations among his friends and admirers, there was much speculation. If Bercovitch had stayed in Munich, had never married, had stayed with Baila, had gone to Paris, had gone to New York, had given himself to a dealer, had never left Bryna, then it all would have been very different.

And so it might have been.

Yet there was greatness both in his life and in his passing. Stubborn, inarticulate, and often the architect of his own pain, he had refused to accept the universe on any terms except his own. He had lived with only one purpose, to be "Alexander Bercovitch — Artist", and to that imperative he had willingly sacrificed not only others but also himself. He died without recognition, treasure, or the comforting presence of his children. He died heavy with neglect and poverty and disappointment.

But he had painted in cities and in deserts, amidst tumult and in tranquillity, in opera houses and in ambitious living-rooms. Forsaking all others, he had followed his one true mistress faithfully for more than fifty years.

Few can say as much.

1. The new building at 5500 Westbury Avenue was officially dedicated on 14 May 1950. See *History of the Montreal YM-YWHA 1910-1985,* ed. Sherry Stein (Montreal : YM-YWHA & NHS Printing, 1985), p. 14.

2. According to Saul Shapiro, a long-time collector of Bercovitch's work, interviewed in Montreal, 20 January 1987, Bercovitch felt hurt that he was always asked to donate his work to bazaars etc. for a Jewish community who had failed to visit him in any significant numbers when he was twice hospitalized. (A Bercovitch landscape, in the collection of Gerry and Morris Krantzberg and shown to the author 17 February 1988, was originally won by Mrs. Krantzberg's uncle in a charity raffle in 1943.)

3. Harold B. Gordon, 23 years old in 1951, interviewed in Montreal 14 January 1987, is the younger brother of Jack J. Gordon, Bercovitch's friend and former student. A poet rather than a painter, he became an unpaid and unofficial secretary to Bercovitch in 1948.

4. Dr. Stern, interviewed in Montreal, 1 December 1986, came to work for Rose Millman at the Dominion Gallery in 1942. He became a partner in 1943, and the sole owner in 1947. He moved the Montreal gallery from Ste. Catherine Street West to its present location on Sherbrooke Street West in 1950. He died in May 1987.

Stern had often taken Bercovitch's work on consignment but had never tried to sell it as aggressively as he had that of Goodridge Roberts, whom Stern put under contract. Bea Bazar, Millman's daughter, interviewed in Montreal, 6 February 1987, believes that Stern was unenthusiastic, at least in part, because Bercovitch had been a favourite of Rose Millman, Stern's predecessor, who had admired his work very much. Stern's only explanation, offered years later, as to why he had not worked more closely with Bercovitch was a cryptic "Bercovitch was his own worst enemy." (In conversation with the author, 1 December 1986.)

5. Stern confirmed this in interview, 1 December 1986.

6. The events are as described by Mrs. Caiserman's daughter, Ghitta, interviewed in Montreal, 9 December 1986.

7. Ruth Pressman, interviewed 19 May and 5 June 1987.

8. Israel Rabinovitch, "Alexander Bercovitch," *Canadian Jewish Chronicle,* 12 January 1951. Also, in Yiddish, in *Der Kanader Adler,* 9 January 1951.

9. Robert Ayre, "Bercovitch Exhibition is Hospitable," *Montreal Star,* 13 January 1951.

10. Jean Dénéchaud, "Une dernière exposition du peintre Alexandre Bercovitch," *La Presse,* 16 January 1951.

11. Rolland Boulanger, "Départ... Alex. Bercovitch," *Arts et Pensée,* 2 (March 1951), p. 52.

12. A.M. Klein, "In Memoriam," *Canadian Jewish Chronicle,* 12 January 1951. Rptd. in *A.M. Klein: Literary Essays and Reviews,* ed. Usher Caplan and M.W. Steinberg (Toronto: U. of Toronto, 1987), p. 199.

13. Inter alia, Adrien Robitaille, "Alexsander Bercovitch," *Le Devoir,* 12 January 1951; "Works by Bercovitch in Snowdon Building," *The Gazette* (Montreal), 13 January 1951; and, later, Moe Reinblatt, "Aleksandre Bercovitch 1893-1951," *Canadian Art,* 8 (Spring 1951), pp. 110-111, and Pearl Leibovitch, "Aleksandre Bercovitch, a Recollection of the Man, the Artist, and the Teacher," *Canadian Jewish Review,* 16 September 1955, pp. 12, 134.

Appendix 1.

*Three letters from David Burliuk
to Alexander Bercovitch*

(All three are addressed to 76 Prince Arthur East, Montreal)
: translated from Russian by Shalom Labkovsky
: author's files

Letter #1. (4 February 1946)

David Burliuk
c/o André Smith
Maitland
Florida

Dear Old Friend,

Please write to me today, tomorrow, without delay, about yourself. Please. As soon as I get your letter, I'll write in detail and mail you some literature.

I was told about you by Gustav, a traveller. Please send me your photo as well as photos of your paintings. Please hurry up and write me. I'll be here three more weeks, and then I'm going south-west.

With friendly greetings,
David Burliuk.

Letter #2. (March 1946)

David Burliuk
Bradenton Beach
Florida

Dear Alexander Bercovitch,

Your letter of 5 March 1946 was forwarded to me in Bradenton Beach, near Sarasota, Florida. I and my wife and son (a veteran of Ocean Village) moved here to the shores of the ocean. Here we'll stay until 26 March, and later we'll move to New York and afterwards to our home on Long Island. "David Burliuk, Hampton Bays, Long Island, N.Y." This is the permanent address.

I married in 1912, and I have two sons, thirty and thirty-two, Nikita and David. The first one was in the war for forty months, and the second for thirty-five months. The first in Europe and the second in New Guinea.

For the first seventeen years, America didn't recognize me. Now, whatever I paint is being sold, and I'm able to devote myself to the arts without having to worry about earnings. This address, "Quebec", is it your permanent one or are you here only temporarily? In June I could fly with my wife to Canada to do some painting for a month. Please write me. I would value your advice. I'm interested in old French Canada. I should know your permanent address. My gallery in New York is "ACA, 63 East 57th. St., (Mr. Herman Baron, art dealer)." When I know your permanent address, I'll mail you a book about me with fifty-three photos of my paintings. I'm sending you now a booklet with a photo of my painting "The Children of Stalingrad" (50" x 86").

I have been in Florida since 20 January 1946. My show in New York was from 15 December 1945 to 1 January 1946. In Cleveland, 20 November until 10 December 1945. The exhibitions were a success. Everything was sold. Write about yourself.

I left Russia 1 April 1918 from Moscow. In October 1920 from Vladivostok to Japan. In August 1922 from Kobé, through Canada, I arrived with my family in New York.

Please write in detail about yourself.
David.

Letter #3. (12 February 1948)

David Burliuk
Bradenton Beach
(After 1 April, Hampton Bays
Long Island
N.Y.

or

2575 Bedford Ave.
Brooklyn, 26
N.Y.)

Dear Friend,

Please sit at your desk and write me a friendly letter about yourself, your work, your health, and so on. I'll manage to get your letter. In my exhibition, the eighth since 1941 in the ACA galleries, my dealer had a big success, as earlier. All the paintings have been sold. Here I paint flowers. I'm longing to see you amid the ocean and the palms.
David Burliuk

Appendix 2.

"Reflections by Bryna Bercovitch," *Der Kanader Adler,* 21 December 1949. Translated from the Yiddish by Sylvia Ary.

It was the summer of the year 1920. In a rainy dawn, I quietly knocked on my mother's door. I had been wounded and was returning home on leave from the Soviet-Polish front. When my mother opened the door she saw a strange figure in a soldier's shirt, with a shaven head, the left arm slung in a black kerchief. She recoiled in horror from the emaciated body and the woebegone face.

"No, it's not Bryna: it's not my child!"

Later we both sat by the boiling samovar. We were drinking tea, having a bite, and talking. With my mother's help I had washed and changed into clean clothing. My mother was already calmer. Sorrowfully, she shook her head.

"Is this, my daughter, what your Revolution does to people?"

I answered, "My revolution is also your revolution, mama. It's the revolution of all hard-working people. In a year — and another year — the revolution, like a mighty fire, will engulf the whole world. You say 'wounds, suffering, bloodshed,' but, mama, you know how hard it is to give birth to a child. How much harder it is for a whole new world to be born. Yes, mama, we will create a new, good, beautiful world. No more war, no more hunger, no more prisons. Mankind will be free and happy — in the near future.

But you don't believe! You're smiling ironically!"

"No, my child, I don't believe, and I am smiling through the pain. Do you know why? I see with whom you're going to be dealing. With Vanka and Stepanka [any Tom, Dick and Harry] you won't create a new world. Only with good people can you establish a good world, and the good are like a drop in the ocean of the bad. So what can you accomplish? Even if there were another thousand like you — oh, I wish that what I'm saying weren't true: I don't even want it to pass my lips!"

A month later, I was already on another front in a Red Army unit, fighting with a group around Kiev. When I returned in wintertime to Kiev and came back to my old quarters in the students' residence, the commandant handed me a letter.

My brother had written me, "Sit shiva, my sister, because our dear mother died at Hanakah, on the third day. She was very lonely for you and until the last minute she worried about you. Dear sister! May God protect you and have pity on us because here where we are there is a terrible hunger. People are dying like flies."

Appendix 3.

"Reflections by Bryna Bercovitch — Part II," *Der Kanader Adler,* 21 December 1949. Translated from the Yiddish by Sylvia Ary.

In the year 1924, Tashkent, Samarkand, Ashkabad, and other cities of the Soviet Orient were flooded with thousands and thousands of homeless boys. Like locusts they would descend on a city and they would terrorise the whole population. In the daytime they would lie hidden in abandoned ruins or in broken waggons behind hills and in ditches, keeping in small groups. At night they would come out of their hiding-places and they would do terrible things. Not only did these homeless ones steal, rob, and rape, but in many cases they also stabbed and shot people. Among these "boys" there were 18-, 20-, and even 30-year old criminals with police records from before the Revolution. They were the ones who were the leaders and guides of the small fry. The Party organization and the Education Commissariat of Ashkabad had to work very hard before they managed to get this mob under control. They mobilised the bravest and most fearless Party people, teachers and workers. Using tact and the best pedagogical methods, they had to round up all these homeless ones in the city and persuade them to enter voluntarily "the colony for homeless boys".

A group of 30 people joined this committee and I was one of them. We were supposed to bring these delinquents back to the right path. It would take too long to tell everything we tried to win their trust. The fact is that, for all our efforts, we always failed. The birds were wary of the net. The homeless ones rarely entered even the city soup-kitchen, although we promised the best beefsteaks and as many por-tions as they wanted. It was very hard to approach their hiding-places. Every time they saw us, they threw stones or mud. They even shot at us several times with pistols.

It was the end of October. The Turkestan winter was heavy rain with cold winds. Once, at a time when the rain had let up a little, we, a group of six comrades, left the city and went to the ruins of Ametchet. We set out early in the evening, hoping to find the "hunters" before they left for the hunt.

As we came close to the place, one comrade lit a torch and we started to sing a revolutionary song. From the ruins there came a few shots. We went on, shouting with all our strength, "Children, don't shoot us, we are your friends. Children, you're living now like dogs, in wet burrows. We will give you a warm home, good food, boots, and clothing. And a school to learn in. Boys — comrades — let us come over. We want to talk with you."

A hail of stones, peel, and sand flew over our heads or into our eyes. But we were determined to get to these people. Bent over, we crawled on all fours up to the entrance. The figures of the boys, lit up by the torch, appeared grotesque. Like monkeys, they leaped across the stone walls. With fearful speed they moved among those frightening ruins, whist-ling, howling, screeching in all languages. But the famous Russian "blessing" ["fornicate with your mother"] rang out sharper and clearer than all the other expressions. It took us several difficult hours before we captured this fortress! The three men of our group had taken off their jackets and given them to the leaders. We, the three women, had wrapped a couple of naked children in our shawls and under-shirts. We kept telling the group that they would have a good life if they came to the colony, and that, if they didn't like it, they would be completely free to leave. We used all kinds of pedagogical ways to influence them and we were successful.

The grey dawn rising over Ashkabad saw the following picture. Over the narrow, muddy streets there marched a regiment of the strangest and most amazing appearance. The three happy male comrades, exhausted and pale but with victorious smiles on their lips, are leading the army of homeless boys into the Persian bath-house. And the three female comrades are racing along in a horse-drawn buggy into the colony to bring back to the bath-house underclothes and boots for the boys.

There comes along an old Turkoman on a donkey. He was hurrying somewhere with a milkchurn. He stopped his donkey and gazed with great amazement at this strange group. In a high-pitched voice he sang out, "Allah! Allah!" Maybe the old Turkoman's "Allah! Allah!" meant the same as the words of my mother (may she rest in peace), "I hope that what I'm saying isn't true, and I don't even want it to pass my lips." Maybe, maybe. But what did they both mean? This I understood only much later and, as they say in the stories, what happened later we'll see afterwards.

Appendix 4.

1926 passport in Turkish, Russian, and French
(front)

1926 passport (back)

Appendix 5.

"Reynald"*, "Aleksander Bercovitch," *La Presse,* 4 January 1934.
(Author's translation)

Aleksander Bercovitch is the painter whose 'discovery' was a sensation last year in Montreal. Born in Kherson, near Odessa, he pursued his artistic studies in Moscow and Leningrad before leaving to roam across Asia. Sidney Carter's establishment 'launched' his work last year — yellow and green faces, highly decorative colour, strange motifs. It was all as Slav-Oriental as one could wish, and more Slav than Oriental, perhaps. His portraits of little girls, shown recently at the Academy Fall Exhibition, seemed to us unpolished and very unsophisticated. What therefore might we expect at the Bercovitch exhibition at Eaton's?

To my surprise, there is no more roughness in the work, no more excessive violence of colour — although in the process the artist may have lost some of those strong characteristics I like to see in painters. I think he made a choice, to put beauty ahead of creativity. Here, this week, you will see above all a Canadianised Bercovitch. It is a masterly choice of subjects, all painted in situ with a sure touch, with no distraction, and with a vibrant but gentle colour. The watercolours are highly finished: the oils are done with strong but harmonious strokes. One has the impression of completion.

There are scenes of harbours bathed in soft light, and joyful landscapes with leafy paths under rose-coloured clouds. But Bercovitch is above all a painter of the city; winter streets with poles, people, and cars all framed in snow or melting into blue shadows; evening scenes with lighted windows in the darkness; Laurier Avenue, for example, crowded with colours, signs, reflections, and passers-by. Such scenes come to life before your eyes without the least excess of detail and with a rare integrity. The experienced control of colour contributes a great deal.

That part of the exhibition given over to the work from Asia is not the least interesting. In such subjects as a striking, fierce, Turkoman face, a mosque drenched in soft light, a market scene, a sunset of a hundred colour harmonies, Bercovitch shows both his Slav virility and his Oriental joy in colour. However interesting his Canadian works may be — and they are very interesting — I will always prefer, from a Slav-Oriental like Bercovitch, those Slav-Oriental works that are truer to his personality. This is my choice in spite of my own Western perception which must always stand in the way of a full understanding of such an artist, and even in spite of my profound misgivings about the way that allegedly foreign influences are luring certain of my compatriots into executing unsightly work.

Bercovitch shows a rare ability to adapt. It is that quality which identifies him as a Semite.

---

* E.R. Bertrand

Appendix 6.

"Pictures by A. Bercovitch Make a Good Show," *Montreal Star,* 27 December 1933. Unsigned, but probably by Robert Ayre.

A small collection of the work of Aleksander Bercovitch was shown at Sidney Carter's gallery last season. It contained some remarkable Oriental studies of places and men and some very interesting decorative designs, mostly formed from oriental ideas. Some works of the same kind are shown again in the larger collection which is now to be seen at Eaton's gallery, with a number of pictures and sketches made in Montreal and its neighbourhood, and, all together, they give a far better impression of Mr. Bercovitch's unusual abilities.

The oriental pictures, mostly in water colour or tempera, are of fine effects of the colour and form of buildings in Bokhara, Ashkabad, and other places in central Asia, and of strong portrait studies of natives of that part of the world. Completely contrasted with these, but quite as good, are the Canadian pictures, mostly oil paintings. These are freely and boldly painted studies of atmosphere, light, and reflections in streets and woods and on ships in Montreal harbour and they show another side of the painter's skill. One picture, called "Gray Day", has a striking effect of distance and atmosphere on a green hillside with rocks; "L'automne passe", which hangs next to it, also has delightful colour and atmosphere and the simplicity of the means in both pictures is surprising. Several little studies called "Summer" are very good and especially one of reflections on a wet pavement, and there are several good tree studies. Some of the street pictures have excellent effects of splashes of light falling through trees on buildings and there is a good sketch of a street under snow. The harbour pictures show the same feeling for light and its reflections and the forms of the ships make fine effects. Of a different kind is "The Day's Ending", a very striking picture of strong green trees seen against a vivid pink sky: yet another picture which is full of light and warmth is a large view of an eastern verandah.

Appendix 7.

Henri Girard, "Alexandre Bercovitch à la galerie Eaton," *Le Canada,* 5 January 1934. (Author's translation.)

Passing through Montreal, Samuel Butler saw a statue of the Discobolus at the back of a shop. It was pushed to one side and covered in dust and cobwebs. You know his exquisitely cruel lines:

'Stowed away in a Montreal lumber-room,
The Discobolus standeth and turneth his face to
    the wall:
Dusty, cobweb-covered, and set at naught.
Beauty crieth in an attic and no man regardeth.
    O God! O Montreal!'

Continuing in this strain, Butler rails at our 'materialist spirit'. Some would chafe at this insolence. I rejoice in it. Would that there were more such chance encounters to penetrate our thick skins! They might one day drag us out of our comfortable lethargy. If we woke up to the reality of Beauty, we would have the Coburns and the Carons put away their tired nags, and, dazzled by a new light, we would become aware of the weariness of our mediocrity.

    O God! O Montreal!

At the present time, if some brave soul from home or abroad tries to show us the simple truth of Life and Nature, avoiding banality, convention, and prejudice, we ignore him or we sneer at him. We haven't yet arrived at that happy point where we will at least see the extent of our ignorance. On the contrary, we see ourselves as very knowledgeable, especially if we have a diploma that gives us the official right to know nothing about everything. And our abominable presumption builds an iron wall around us which is impervious to the heroic efforts of Jules Fournier.

You take my point? I was getting angry. Some obscure instinct made me get this preamble off my chest before I begin to praise the work of a foreign painter, Alexandre Bercovitch, presently exhibiting at Eaton's Gallery.

'To take to your use out of the compact cities as
    you pass through,
  To carry buildings and streets with you afterward
    wherever you go.'

One might say that Bercovitch was guided by Walt Whitman's injunction when he left his Russian home and went to Asia. Intoxicated with youth, his eyes craving new sights, he went to find his Muse under different skies. Turkestan, Armenia, Persia — no more than carpet-makers to us — showed him the poetry and the unknown riches of their civilizations. In Bokhara, in the "kibitka" of a nomad, he heard the minstrel sing of the glory of Turkoman heroes, of the grandeur of freedom, and of the love of love. The artist surrendered to the light and the atmosphere of this sun-filled country. He took note of the architecture, and felt at one with the landscape. But, everywhere, he found the underlying truth of reality. He was not just a traveller, greedy for new sensations. Alexandre Bercovitch is, above all else, dedicated to authentic expression, visual truth, and harmony of colour. Guided by the same Muse he had in the East, he has just discovered America. I will not say that he seeks an insight: rather I will say that he finds it, makes it part of himself, and then presents it to us. The insight is all the more moving for having passed through the artist's inner being. It is strange to see Montreal in this way, through the eyes of Mr.

Bercovitch. A sad spectacle, and yet so true. Under the snow, the rain, or the sun, Montreal acquires a kind of tragic grandeur. There is a feeling of distress. We feel touched, as if we have seen a close relative in a wretched state. Similarly, we realize that our delight in his Eastern work cannot therefore come from mere surprise at the unfamiliar, but must derive from the artist's unique way of seeing and feeling, of bringing from the depth of his being the passion for life that we see in his work. It is hard to define. I would say that the work of Alexandre Bercovitch appears as the 'confession' of an exceptional eye.

A certain stylisation shows the Asiatic influence, but there is a subtlety and refinement, an indefinable charm, in the work of Mr. Bercovitch which is the unmistakeable stamp of Paris. I was looking for the precise way to convey this impression when the painter, as if reading my mind, admitted to his admiration for French civilization and French art. Russian collections have some of the best of Manet, Renoir, Dégas, Monet, and Cézanne. It was Bercovitch's fate to study in Munich, but he dreamed of Paris. It is therefore natural that a French soul, even one deformed in Montreal, should experience an empathy with Bercovitch's work, a work which vibrates with the desire to commune with a fellow French spirit. J.W. Morrice, whom Louis Gillet seems to think is the best of our painters, also makes Paris the lodestone of his artistic pilgrimage. It would be instructive to make a comparison between his work and that of Bercovitch. I can already see a similarity in their ability to express themselves with elegance and clarity, without sinking into affectation.

I will guarantee one thing, the work of Alexandre Bercovitch is never banal. The man has put his emotion into every one of his works, even those which do not quite succeed. If the artist sometimes lacks a little taste — by our Western standards — he is often elevated by unparalleled inspiration. Look carefully at "The Verandah", "The Fir-trees", and "The Turkomen under the Kibitka". The painter's mind seems to be able to see, in a single instant, the authentic inner truth of an object, of a landscape, or of a man, and to capture those qualities and those colours which express that truth in its entirety. I know perfectly well that it doesn't happen quite like that, and that each painting needs preliminary sketches and later careful revisions. But I admire the technical mastery, the discreet know-how, that permits an artist to paint what he pleases without letting the technique become too obvious. I find myself looking at work that owes nothing to pretentiousness or commercialism. Bercovitch's brush refuses the easy repetition that can make an artist's name familiar to a lazy public. His hand does not serve the call of fashion. He does not want the title of 'artist' as it is bestowed by the 'élite' whose sycophants feed them the rose-coloured suavities and saccharin-festivals they crave. For Bercovitch, like Hébert, Humphrey, Smith, Holgate, and, doubtless, some others, we shall have to invent a new title, since 'artist' has become a synonym of 'distinguished dauber'.

The world has many artists, but few are those who see with their own eyes and have the courage to paint what they see. They must also have culture, taste, and a sense of the internal reality of existence — all qualities which are manifest in the work of Alexandre Bercovitch. Should we be surprised that he is not more deservedly known? Bercovitch could say, like Eugène Delacroix, 'I was certainly not born to paint fashionable paintings.'

Bercovitch Exhibitions
After 1926

(solo exhibitions shown with *)

1927 (March 24 — April 18)
Spring Exhibition, Art Association of Montreal.

1928 (March 22 — April 15)
Spring Exhibition, Art Association of Montreal.

1929 (March 21 — April 14)
Spring Exhibition, Art Association of Montreal.

1932 (March 17 — April 17)
Spring Exhibition, Art Association of Montreal.
(October 8-23)
Independent Art Association,
Sun Life Building, Montreal.

1933 (March 16 — April 6)
Spring Exhibition, Art Association of Montreal.
*   (April)
Sidney Carter Studio, Montreal.
(November 16 — December 17)
Royal Canadian Academy Fall Exhibition,
Montreal.
*   (December 27 — January 4)
Eaton's Galleries, Montreal.

1934 (April 19 — May 13)
Spring Exhibition, Art Association of Montreal.
(December)
Massey Collection Exhibition,
Art Gallery of Toronto.

1935 (March 21 — April 4)
Spring Exhibition, Art Association of Montreal.
(May)
Exhibition of Students of Bercovitch,
YWHA, Montreal.
*   (October — November)

Eaton's Galleries, Montreal.
(November)
National "Produced in Canada" Exhibition,
Sun Life Building, Montreal.
(November 21 — December 22)
Royal Canadian Academy Fall Exhibition,
Montreal.

1936 (January)
Canadian Group of Painters, travelling
exhibition, beginning at the Art Gallery
of Toronto.
(March)
Ontario Society of Artists,
Art Gallery of Toronto.
(March 19 — April 12)
Spring Exhibition, Art Association of Montreal.
(April)
"Canadian and European Art,"
Watson Gallery, Montreal.
(May)
"Survey of Canadian Art," W. Scott & Sons
Gallery, Montreal.
(November 6 — December 8)
Royal Canadian Academy Fall Exhibition,
Toronto.
(December)
Students of Bercovitch, YWHA, Montreal.

1937 (February)
Montreal Arts Club (organized by John Lyman).
(March 18 — April 11)
Spring Exhibition, Art Association of Montreal.
(May 8-29)
Artists of British Empire Overseas,
London, U.K.

(July)
W. Scott & Sons Gallery, Montreal.
(October — November)
National "Produced in Canada" Exhibition,
Sun Life Building, Montreal.
(November 18 — December 17)
Royal Canadian Academy Fall Exhibition,
Montreal.

1938 (March)
Ontario Society of Artists,
Art Gallery of Toronto.
(March 17 — April 10)
Spring Exhibition, Art Association of Montreal.
(April 1-19)
W. Scott & Sons Gallery (Auction), Montreal.
(November — December)
Eastern Group, W. Scott & Sons Gallery,
Montreal.
(December)
Exhibition in Aid of Spanish Democracy,
2037 Peel St., Montreal.

1939 (June 10 — July 31)
Canadian Society of Painters in Water-Colour,
New York World's Fair.
(July — August)
Summer Exhibition, Art Association
of Montreal.
(August 25 — September 9)
Canadian National Exhibition, Toronto.
(December 15-30)
Contemporary Arts Society, Stephens Gallery,
Montreal.

1940 (January — February)
Eastern Group, Art Association of Montreal.
(February 2-29)
Canadian Society of Painters in Water-Colour,
Art Gallery of Toronto.
(March 20 — April 14)
Spring Exhibition, Art Association of Montreal.
(November 22 — December 15)
Contemporary Arts Society, Art Association
of Montreal.

1941 (March 20 — April 13)
Spring Exhibition, Art Association of Montreal.

1942 (January)
"Four Artists," Art Gallery of Toronto
Print Room.
(April 1 — April 30)
Spring Exhibition, Art Association of Montreal.

1945 (January — April)
"Development of Painting in Canada,
1665-1945,"
January, Art Gallery of Toronto
February, Art Association of Montreal
March, National Gallery, Ottawa
(organizing gallery)
April, Le Musée de la Province de Québec.

*1945 (November 18 — December 2)
Seminary of Joliette, Québec.

1950 (March 14 — April 9)
Spring Exhibition, Montreal Museum
of Fine Arts (formerly Art Association
of Montreal).
(October 14-31)
"Contemporary Jewish Painters,"
Garfield Gallery, Toronto.

*1951 (January 7 — 24)
YM-YWHA, Montreal.
(March)
"Two Painters; Bercovitch and Watt,"
Montreal Museum of Fine Arts, Gallery XII.

1955 (November 13-27)
"Alexander Bercovitch and Sylvia Ary,"
YM-YWHA, Montreal.

1959 (October 29 — November 15)
"Canadian Jewish Artists," Montreal Museum
of Fine Arts.

1962 (March — April)
"Canadian Jewish Artists," Peretz School,
Vancouver, B.C.

1965 (March 16 — April 3)
Artlenders Gallery, Montreal.

1987 "Jewish Painters and Modernity:
to Montreal 1930-1945,"
1989 (October 6 — November 5)
Saidye Bronfman Centre, Montreal.
(January 10 — February 7)
Sherbrooke University.
(May 4 — June 30)
Koffler Gallery, Toronto.
(September 12 — November 20)
Joliette Art Museum.
(December 15 — February 28, 1989)
University of Saskatchewan.
(March 11 — April 30, 1989)
Edmonton Art Gallery.

130

Bibliography

A. Books

Baron, Salo. *The Russian Jews under Tsars and Soviets.* New York: McMillan, 1976.

Ben-Ari, Raikin. *Habima.* New York: Yoseloff, 1957.

Betcherman, Lita-Rose. *The Swastika and the Maple Leaf: Fascist Movements in Canada in the Thirties.* Toronto: Fitzhenry and Whiteside, 1975.

Bonneville, Jean-Pierre. *Marc-Aurèle Fortin en Gaspésie.* Montréal: Stanké, 1980.

Buckle, Richard. *Diaghilev.* London: Hamish Hamilton, 1979.

Cooper, Douglas. *The Cubist Epoch.* New York: Dutton, 1970.

Davitt, Michael. *Within the Pale.* Philadelphia: Jewish Publication Society of America, 1903.

Dube, Wolf-Dieter. *Expressionism.* Trans. Mary Whittall. New York: Praeger, 1973.

Duval, Paul. *Four Decades: the Canadian Group of Painters and their Contemporaries, 1930-1970.* Toronto: Clarke-Irwin, 1972.

Dyonnet, Edmond. *Mémoires d'un artiste canadien.* Ottawa: les éditions de l'université d'Ottawa, 1968.

Figler, Bernard and Rome, David. *Hannaniah Meir Caiserman: a Biography.* Montreal: Northern Printing, 1962.

Gilbert, Martin. *The Jews of Russia.* London: National Council for Soviet Jewry, 1976.

Gray, Camilla. *The Great Experiment: Russian Art 1863-1922.* New York: Abrams, 1962.

Grober, Chayele. *Mein Weg Alein.* Tel Aviv: Perez, 1968.

Haftmann, Werner. *Chagall.* Trans. Heinrich Baumann and Alexis Brown. New York: Abrams, 1984.

Harper, Russell. *La peinture au Canada: des origines à nos jours.* Québec: les presses de l'université de Laval, 1969.

Hart, Arthur ed. *The Jew in Canada.* Toronto: Hunter-Rose, 1926.

History of the Montreal YM-YWHA 1910-1985. Ed. Sherry Stein. Montreal: YM-YWHA & NHS Printing, 1985.

Howe, Irving. *World of our Fathers.* New York: Harcourt, Brace, Jovanovich, 1976.

Jaffe, Hans. *Nineteenth and Twentieth Century Painting.* New York: Dell, 1967.

Jenkins, Kathleen. *Montreal.* New York: Doubleday, 1966.

Jubilee Book: Thirtieth Anniversary of the Russian Polish Hebrew Sick Benefit Association of Montreal. Ed. Myer Fox. Montreal: City Printing Co., 1937.

Kilbourn, Elizabeth. *Great Canadian Painting: a Century of Art.* Toronto: Canadian Centennial Publishing, 1966.

Knott, Leonard L. *Montreal 1900-1930.* Toronto: Nelson, Foster, and Scott, 1976.

Kuhns, William and Rosshandler, Léo. *Sam Borenstein.* Toronto: McClelland and Stewart, 1978.

Lamonde, Yvan and Trépanier, Esther. *L'avènement de la modernité culturelle au Québec.* Montréal: Institut Québécois de Recherche sur la Culture, 1986.

Langlais, Jacques and Rome, David. *Juifs et québécois français.* Montréal: Fidès, 1986.

Lifar, Serge. *A History of the Russian Ballet.* Trans. A. Haskell. London: Hutchison, 1954.

Lord, Barry. *The History of Painting in Canada: Towards a People's Art.* Toronto: N.C. Press, 1974.

McDougall, Anne. *Anne Savage: The Story of a Canadian Painter.* Montreal: Harvest House, 1977.

McInnes, Graham. *Canadian Art.* Toronto: McMillan, 1950.

Reid, Dennis. *A Concise History of Canadian Painting.* Toronto: Oxford U.P., 1973.

Robert, Guy. *Fortin: l'œuvre et l'homme.* Montréal: les éditions France-Amérique, 1982.

_____. *La peinture au Québec depuis ses origines.* Ste. Adèle, Qué.: Iconia, 1978.

Secunda, Victoria. *Bei Mihr Bist Du Schon: the Life of Sholom Secunda.* New York: Magic Circle Press, 1982.

Shoolman, Regina and Slatkin, Charles. *Enjoyment of Art in America.* New York: Lippincott, 1942.

Teboul, Victor. *Mythe et images du Juif au Québec.* Montréal: Éditions de Lagrave, 1977.

Whitford, Frank. *Kandinsky.* New York: Hamlyn, 1967.

B. Articles

Aubin, Réal. "Une exposition des peintures d'Alexandre Bercovitch." *Le Séminaire de Joliette.* 10 (1945), p. 10.

Ayre, Robert. "Art in Montreal is Given New and Vigorous Life." *Saturday Night,* 16 November 1940, p. 19.

_____. "'Art of our Day' Attracting Attention by its Vigour in Design." *The Standard,* 20 May 1939.

_____. "Bercovitch Exhibition is Hospitable." *Montreal Star,* 13 January 1951.

_____. "'Fundamental' and Other Views on Canvas: Second Thoughts on Canadian Group Show." *The Standard,* 13 January 1940.

_____. "Review of Fine Arts Museum Show." *Montreal Star,* 24 March 1951.

_____. "The Eastern Group Has a Show." *Saturday Night,* 17 December 1938, p. 36.

Balfour, Lisa. "Artlenders Exhibition." *Montreal Star,* 20 March 1965.

Booker, Bertram. "The Seven Arts." *The Citizen* (Ottawa), 29 December 1928.

Boulanger, Rolland. "Départ... Alex. Bercovitch." *Arts et Pensée,* 2 (March 1951), p. 52.

Caiserman, H.M. "The Art of Bercovitch and Muhlstock." *The Jewish Standard,* 14 April 1933, pp. 169-170.

Dénéchaud, Jean. "Une dernière exposition du peintre Alexandre Bercovitch." *La Presse,* 16 January 1951.

Forster, Michael. "A. Bercovitch, R. Watt Paintings at Museum," *The Standard,* 24 March 1951.

Girard, Henri. "Alexandre Bercovitch à la galerie Eaton." *Le Canada,* 5 January 1934.

_____. "Des oeuvres et une opinion." *Le Canada,* 25 January 1939.

_____. "Des peintres canadiens." *Le Canada,* 20 August 1937.

_____. "Fritz Brandtner à la galerie Henry Morgan." *Le Canada,* 26 February 1936.

_____. "L'art." *Le Canada,* 30 October 1935.

_____. "L'école de Paris." *Le Canada,* 22 October 1936.

_____. "Le mois artistique." *Le Canada,* 1 March 1933.

_____. "Le salon du printemps." *Le Canada,* 5 April 1935.

Harrison, Allan. "Artists Thrown into Discard." (Letter to the editor) *Montreal Star,* 30 December 1972.

Harvey, Jean-Charles. "Le pire obstacle à l'art canadien." *Le Jour,* 1, No. 28 (26 March 1938).

Klein, A.M. "In Memoriam." *Canadian Jewish Chronicle,* 12 January 1951. Rptd. in *A.M. Klein: Literary Essays and Reviews.* Ed. Usher Caplan and M.W. Steinberg. Toronto: U. of Toronto, 1987, pp.198-199.

Lanken, Dane. "The Reign of the 'Queens' Draws to a Close." *The Gazette* (Montreal), 13 October 1973.

Leibovitch, Pearl. "Aleksandre Bercovitch, a Recollection of the Man, the Artist, the Teacher." *Canadian Jewish Review,* 16 September 1955, pp. 12, 134.

Lemieux, Jean-Paul. "La peinture chez les canadiens-français." *Le Jour,* 1, No. 44 (16 July 1938).

Lyman, John. "Letter to the Editor." *Canadian Forum,* 12, No. 140 (May 1932), p. 313.

_____. "The Canadian Group." *The Montrealer,* 1 February 1938.

Neumann, Ernst. "Jewish Artists." *Canadian Jewish Year Book 1940-1941,* ed. Vladimir Grossman. Montreal: Woodward, 1940, pp. 172-179.

Ostry, Ethel. "Jewish Social Welfare in Canada." *Canadian Jewish Year Book 1939-1940,* ed. Vladimir Grossman. Montreal: Woodward, 1939, pp. 102-105.

Rabinovitch, Israel. "Yiddish Theatre in Montreal." *Canadian Jewish Year Book 1940-1941,* ed. Vladimir Grossman. Montreal : Woodward, 1940, pp. 166-171.

_____. "Alexander Bercovitch." *Canadian Jewish Chronicle,* 12 January 1951. The tribute was also published in Yiddish in *Der Kanader Adler,* 9 January 1951.

Reinblatt, Moe. "Aleksandre Bercovitch 1893-1951." *Canadian Art,* 8 (Spring 1951), pp. 110-111.

_____. "Distilled a Lot of Art." *Canadian Jewish Outlook,* December 1966, p. 12.

"Reynald" (E.R. Bertrand). "Aleksander Bercovitch." *La Presse,* 4 January 1934.

_____. "Bercovitch n'a pas trahi Percé." *La Presse,* 2 November 1935.

_____. "Élèves de Bercovitch." *La Presse,* 19 December 1936.

_____. "Les cauchemars de Fritz Brandtner." *La Presse,* 22 February 1936.

_____. "Les inspirations du milieu social." *La Presse,* 20 February 1935.

_____. "Rappel Bercovitch." *La Presse,* 9 November 1935.

_____. "Réintroduction au modernisme." *La Presse,* 9 October 1937.

Robitaille, Adrien. "Alexsander Bercovitch." *Le Devoir,* 12 January 1951.

Sabbath, Lawrence. "Goodridge Roberts Comes into Perspective." *The Gazette* (Montreal), 27 August 1983.

Shoolman, Regina. "Aleksandre Bercovitch Acclaimed by Art Lovers." *Canadian Jewish Review.* 7 April 1933.

Wood, Elizabeth Wyn. "Art and the Pre-Cambrian Shield." *Canadian Forum,* 16, No. 193 (February 1937), pp. 13-15.

C. Unsigned articles

"Bercovitch Shows Paintings of Gaspé." *The Gazette* (Montreal), 4 November 1935.

"Creations of Jewish Artists on Display." *Canadian Jewish Chronicle,* 30 March 1962.

"Dr. Max Stern." *The Gazette* (Montreal), 30 May 1987.

"Eviction of Artist Brings Recognition." *Montreal Daily Herald.* 7 April 1933.

"Funeral Set Today of A. Bercovitch, Montreal Painter." *The Gazette* (Montreal), 9 January 1951.

"Late A. Bercovitch Paintings on View." *The Gazette* (Montreal), 24 March 1951.

"Le peintre Bercovitch est mort à 59 ans." *La Patrie,* 9 January 1951.

"M. A. Bercovitch décédé à 60 ans." *La Presse,* 9 January 1951.

"Pictures by A. Bercovitch Make a Good Show." *Montreal Star,* 27 December 1933.

"Pictures of Sea by A. Bercovitch Make Fine Display." *Montreal Star,* 30 October 1935.

"Works by Bercovitch in Snowdon Building." *The Gazette* (Montreal), 13 January 1951.

D. Catalogues of major exhibitions

Art Association of Montreal. *Spring Exhibitions, 1926-1951.*

Barnett, Vivian Endicott. *Kandinsky at the Guggenheim.* New York : Abbeville, 1983.

Canadian Group of Painters. Toronto : Art Gallery of Toronto, 1936.

Hill, Charles. *Canadian Painting in the Thirties.* Ottawa : National Gallery, 1975.

Montreal Museum of Fine Arts. *Exhibition of Works by Canadian Jewish Artists,* October-November, 1959.

Royal Canadian Academy. *November Exhibitions,* 1933, 1935, 1936, 1937.

"The Development of Painting in Canada." *Catalogue of 1945 Exhibition* at Art Gallery of Toronto (Jan.), Art Association of Montreal (Feb.), National Gallery (March), and Le Musée de la province de Québec (April). Toronto : Ryerson, 1945.

The McMichael Canadian Collection. Preface Rosemary Shipton. Toronto : Cook, 1983.

Trépanier, Esther. *Jewish Painters and Modernity : Montreal 1930-1945.* Montreal : Saidye Bronfman Centre, 1987.

Varley, Christopher. *The Contemporary Arts Society.* Edmonton : Edmonton Art Gallery, 1980.

Wilkin, Karen. *Goodridge Roberts : Selected Works : a Touring Exhibition.* Saskatoon : Mendel Art Gallery, 1981.

E. General reference works

Canadian Jewish Year Book 1939-1940. Ed. Vladimir Grossman. Montreal : Woodward, 1939.

Canadian Jewish Year Book 1940-1941. Ed. Vladimir Grossman. Montreal : Woodward, 1940.

Dictionary of Twentieth-Century Art. New York : Phaedon, 1973.

Encyclopaedia Britannica, 1926 and 1974.

Encyclopaedia Judaica, 1971.

Encyclopaedia of World Art. New York: McGraw-Hill, 1967.

Hamilton, George Heard. *Pelican History of Art: Painting and Sculpture in Europe, 1880-1940.* London: Penguin, 1967.

MacDonald, Colin S. *A Dictionary of Canadian Artists.* Ottawa: Canadian Paperbacks, 1967.

The Oxford Companion to Twentieth Century Art. Ed. Harold Osborne. New York: Oxford U.P., 1981.

F. Various

Downes, Lionel Fielding. "A. Bercovitch." An unpublished and undated memoir.

Garmaise, Eudice. "39 Prints — the opening address." Speech delivered at the opening of an exhibition of Québec art at the University of Edinburgh's Canada Studies Week, 1977.

Guide to the Montreal Museum of Fine Arts, 1977.

Kalman Barkov. A memorial book published by his friends, Jerusalem, 1950.

National Gallery of Canada Biographical Information Forms. Submitted to the Gallery by Alexander Bercovitch in May 1932 and in June 1942.

Perrault, Lise. Interviews with Paul Dumas (26 March 1973), Allan Harrison (22 March 1973), and Philip Surrey (28 March 1973). Conducted under direction of Professor François-Marc Gagnon as part of graduate research. Files of Art History Department, l'Université de Montréal.